Welcome to
The Staggered Groom Guide

In case you didn't know **www.iamstaggered.com** is the UK's leading men's wedding website. We're sure we're leading because we're also the only men's wedding website. Fortunately for you, we're also brilliant and as this publication proves we make wedding planning easy for blokes. Whether it's suits, speeches, stag dos or even floristry – Staggered can help you sort it.

And make no mistake, men are getting involved with weddings in a big way now. There are mainstream (well, BBC3) TV programmes about grooms taking complete control of the wedding planning. Wedding suppliers are reporting that the groom is taking a lead role in making decisions about the wedding. Best of all, **www.iamstaggered.com** now gets over 40,000 men a month reading the site and has a membership of more than 30,000 grooms, best men and fathers of the bride.

Our work here is not done. There is so much more we're looking forward to achieving, and top of that list is helping you to have a great wedding. So if you're a groom, best man or father of the bride then this publication is your essential guide. It's crammed with wedding planning ideas you can pass off as your own (and take the credit for, obviously) and easy-to-follow advice about getting the best of everything. We've solved the most common problems, given you the insider knowledge and showcased the most stylish grooms who have been there, done that and got the tailored shirt to prove it.

Whatever role you're taking in the wedding planning – from laid-back to fully engaged - we promise that between this publication and **www.iamstaggered.com** you will be 100% prepared.

Now let's get to work.
Staggered

What's inside

The Staggered Groom Guide covers everything you need to know if you're a groom, a best man or a father of the bride.

It's compiled by the team at **www.iamstaggered.com**, the UK's leading men's wedding website. Every month over 40,000 men trust Staggered to help them prepare for their wedding.

The Staggered Groom Guide is the only publication you'll need to help you cope with the wedding, but if you want anything else then get in touch.

Get in touch

Find us on **www.iamstaggered.com**
email us **info@iamstaggered.com**
or pick up the phone **0844 310 4050** (local rate)
we're also on Twitter at **@iamstaggered**
and **www.facebook.com/iamstaggered**

Join Staggered

It's free, you get to post on the forum, you get our emails, access to a range of exclusive discounts and you get free anniversary reminders for life. Sign up at **www.iamstaggered.com.**

Made by:

The wonderful team of Craig Morris, Yolander Yeo, Andrew Shanahan, Emma Shanahan, Mark Hooson, Brenda Della Casa, Helen O'Connor, Bernice de Braal and Dan Stubbs.

Real Grooms

Throughout The Staggered Groom Guide, you'll find our series of Real Grooms who have been there and done that. Don't forget to steal their style, their stag ideas and benefit from their advice.

weddings | blokes | sorted

With thanks to:

Five things every
groom should know

1

The wedding is not just the bride's big day

Now we're not stupid (ok, we're a bit stupid) and we know that you haven't been obsessing about your wedding day since you were a child like the bride has, but we also know that it is still one of the most important days in your life and you want it to be perfect. In our view the wedding should be the best party the bride and groom can throw to celebrate them and their relationship. Despite what the occasional mother-in-law might say – that means it's essential that the groom is involved every bit as much as the bride.

2

You're about to face some unique problems

Unless you're reading this for advance planning then you'll probably already have confronted the issue of how to propose. But unless you're made of iron, like that iron man from that film, then there's a good chance that you'll be having some wedding-related nerves from now on. Whether it's cold feet, hating being at the centre of attention, not getting along with your mother-in-law or fretting about your speech or first night sex, never feel like you're the only one to feel like this. Have a look at **www.iamstaggered.com/ wedding-nerves**

3

Perfect planning prevents poor performance

Let's be frank: the more you help out with the wedding planning, the more control you can have over the day itself. Plus your wife-to-be will think you're great. This includes how much it costs and what actually happens. Trust us on this – doing a bit of work is way better than the alternative, where you turn up wearing a suit you hate, speak to people you don't know and have a day that does nothing to celebrate who you are as a couple.

4

Think big and think independently

Don't be afraid to go big with the wedding; yes it's essential that you pick a budget you can afford and stick to it, but don't be afraid to express what you want. If you've always wanted to have a plane draw your face with smoke in the sky, then your wedding is the time to ask for it. Also, choose your own path - you can get loads of inspiration from other grooms (check out the Real Grooms through the magazine) but be bold and make your own choices.

5

The whole happily ever after business...

Never forget the saying: the wedding is enjoyable, the marriage is important.

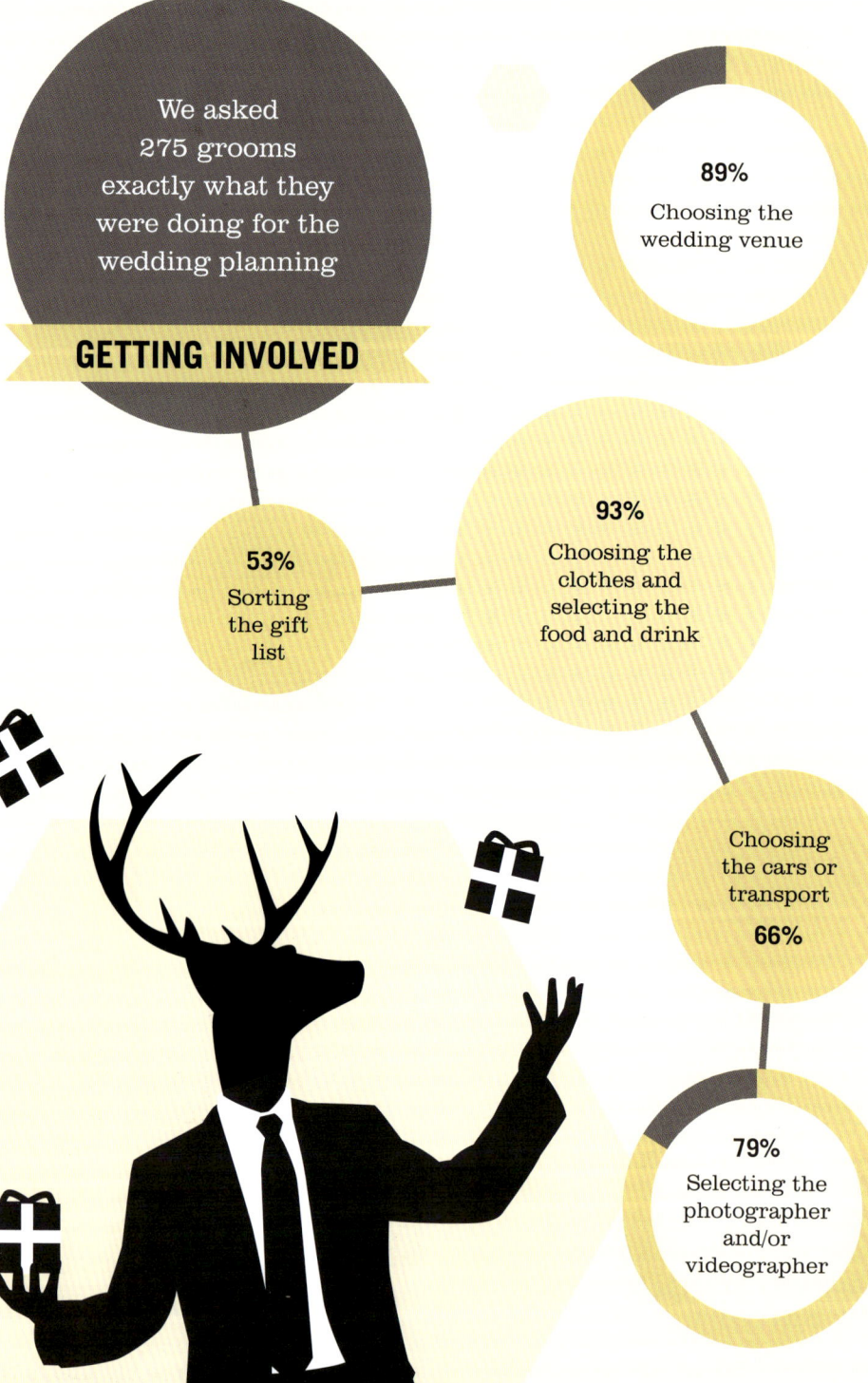

We asked 275 grooms exactly what they were doing for the wedding planning

GETTING INVOLVED

89%
Choosing the wedding venue

93%
Choosing the clothes and selecting the food and drink

53%
Sorting the gift list

Choosing the cars or transport
66%

79%
Selecting the photographer and/or videographer

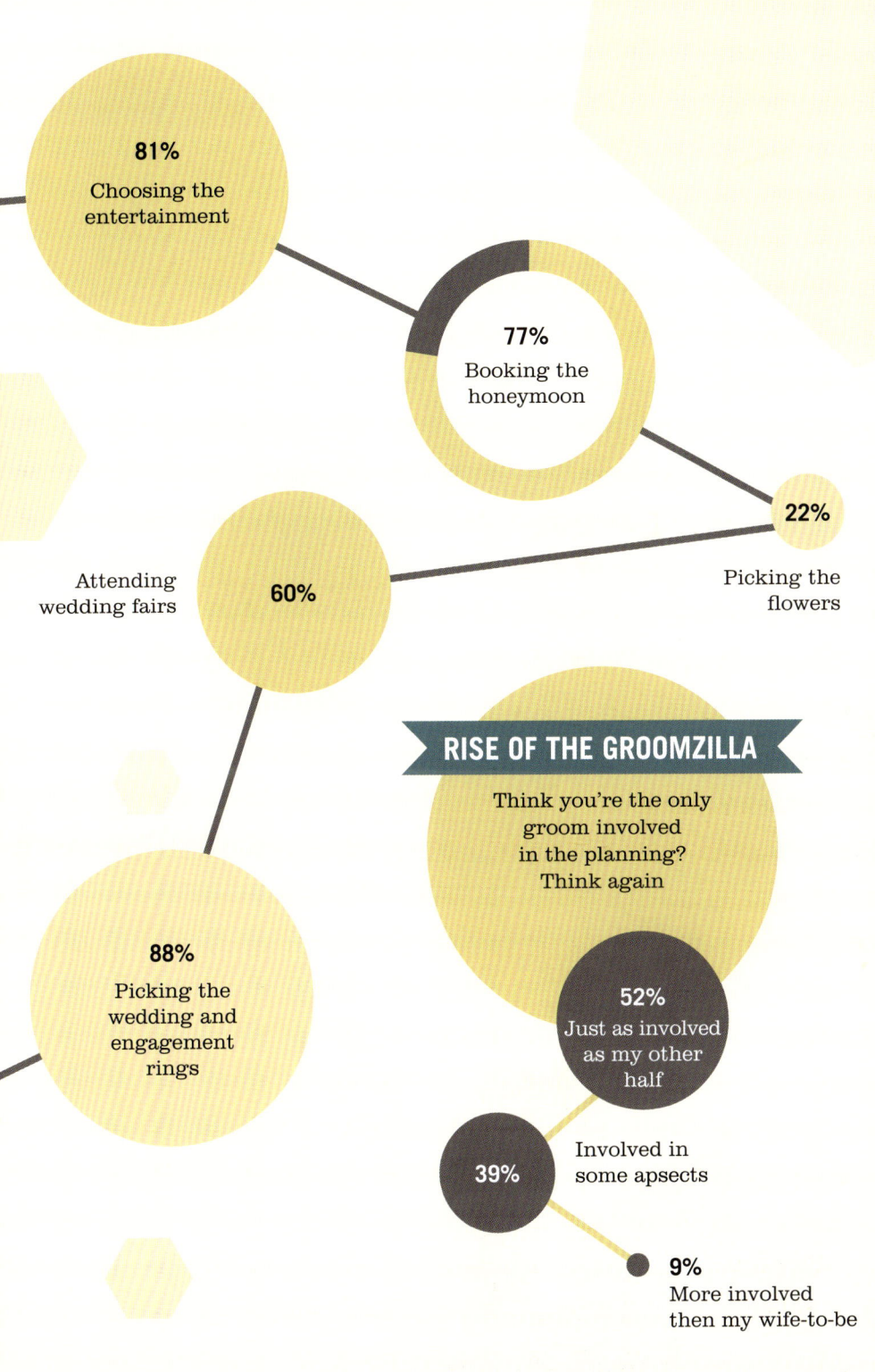

81%
Choosing the
entertainment

77%
Booking the
honeymoon

22%
Picking the
flowers

Attending
wedding fairs

60%

RISE OF THE GROOMZILLA

Think you're the only
groom involved
in the planning?
Think again

88%
Picking the
wedding and
engagement
rings

52%
Just as involved
as my other
half

39%
Involved in
some apsects

9%
More involved
then my wife-to-be

Real Groom

Richard Gordon

Age: 30
Bride's Name: Deborah
Best Man: Paul Charalambous

Where did you get married?
The ceremony was at Park Circus Registrars in Glasgow and our reception was Cail Bruich in Bridge of Weir.

Where was your stag do – any scars?
Our stag was basically ten good friends, we hired a cottage close to Stirling and drank and ate for two full days. It was great catching up with lots of friends from all over the UK that hadn't seen each other for a while. It wasn't mental and nothing 'crazy' really happened on it. Just put on a stone with the drink and food.

What did the men wear on the day?
After much deliberating and trying on suits I finally decided to match Deborah's vintage theme and wear a mod style suit. I bought a Ben Sherman Slim Fit suit and got it all tailored to fit me perfectly, as I am an awkward size and nothing seems to ever fit perfectly on me.

The groomsmen got all their own suits which we requested was any shade of grey. We bought the socks, ties and handkerchiefs for them. Deborah sorted our son Oliver's

outfit; waistcoat, trousers and coat from Debenhams, bow tie and shirt from H&M and we bought him red Converse. The scarf I'm wearing is Deborah's!

What three pieces of advice would you give to blokes going through the whole wedding thing now?
1. Make sure your best man and usher help you throughout the day as there is so much going on, you will forget something.

2. Remember to give your mum flowers when you are doing your speech (as I totally forgot).

3. Just relax as much as you can and try to savour the experience as it passes by quicker than you can ever imagine.

A word for the lady, come on, say something emotional about your bride...
Deborah basically was the wedding – she is an interior designer and she created the whole reception hall and also the room and tables where we had our meal. It was nothing short of spectacular. She also looked absolutely stunning. Without her and her ideas I wouldn't have experienced the most perfect day in my life.

Five things every **best man** should know

1

It's a great honour to be best man but it's also bloody hard work

There's no doubting that being asked to be a best man is a huge honour, but let's not kid ourselves, he (or she) has one of the hardest roles to play at the wedding. You think we're kidding? You've got to organise the most memorable weekend of your best mate's life. You've got to write and deliver a speech that hilariously destroys him but somehow magically doesn't upset anyone. And all that comes before we even mention looking grateful when he gives you your "best man" socks to say thanks. Start here: **www.iamstaggered.com/best-man**

2

The most legendary stag dos need careful planning

It's the groom's momentous goodbye to bachelorhood and it's your responsibility. The first step is working out how to execute the ultimate stag do, so skip ahead to the feature on P44. Please note though that the word "execute" should in no way give you ideas about pranks. If you're looking for help on locations then our stag do City Guides **(www.iamstaggered.com/stag-do-city-guides)** are a good place to start. Also let us do your research, it's completely free and all you have to do is fill in the form at **www.iamstaggered.com/book-your stag-do** and take the credit.

3

Stag dos come in all shapes and sizes (and prices)

What to do on the stag do is the big question. You might fancy sticking with the stag do classics like paintball, a day at the horses, go-karting or a trip to the football, or the classic destinations like Vegas or Amsterdam. Especially in these difficult financial times it's worth bearing in mind that a £100+ stag do can put a lot of pressure on stags so try and have elements people can opt into to save cash, or offer a local do for anyone who can't afford a bigger bash.

4

Your speech should be a personal tribute not a stand-up routine

The greatest best man speeches are a personal tribute to the groom (and also to the bride if you know her well enough), that doesn't mean cheesy jokes, see page 65. The key to sorting out your wedding speech is preparation in advance, soliciting for material from different groups of people and ultimately rejecting the temptation to destroy him – it never, ever ends well.

5

Your role goes beyond a speech and a drinking session

As best man you'll need to be there as an emotional support for the groom – you're obviously very close friends for him to have chosen you – but now more than ever a regular get together to see how he is would be worth organising. You're working hard but he's under a hell of a lot of pressure, so try not to fake sleep when he's off-loading about the wedding.

Real Groom
Dan Woodward

Age: 30

Bride's name: Sharon Woodward

Best man: Barrie Woodward

Where was your stag do – any scars?

No physical scars, but it was touch and go if there was going to be any emotional scars! We went to Thorpe Park in the day which was a lot of fun, but the evening got out of hand and I think a lot of the stress that was built up in the run up to the wedding reared its ugly head. This ended up with me almost getting arrested. Twice. Luckily I had a great best man, who pulled me through it all and ultimately I am better for the experience. One thing I have to say is that I probably built the stag do up too much in my head, and wish I had just relaxed and enjoyed the experience.

Where did you get married?

Nonsuch Mansion in Cheam, Surrey. It's just down the road from our flat in Sutton, and we often go walking in Nonsuch Park where it resides. It's great that we can go and see the venue any time we want. It's an amazing venue, and the staff there are brilliant.

What did the men wear on the day?

All the suits were made by Suitopia. They were all the same style, but mine was cashmere wool, with a custom lining. All the guys had a white shirt of their choice, combined with matching ties from Debenhams. My shirt was a lilac herringbone shirt from Ted Baker with a purple tie from Paul Smith. My shoes were purple suede brogues from Jones the Bootmakers. I made the buttonholes myself, taking a great deal of inspiration from the fabulous designs at Soobird.com

What three pieces of advice would you give to blokes going through the whole wedding thing now?

Write for Staggered – not only is the site an amazing community, but writing a blog is amazingly cathartic. It also opens you up to loads of alternative ideas and experiences, making sure that you question what you really want. I found that our wedding ended up being more of a collaboration between my wife and I, and ultimately was a celebration of our personalities.

Choose your suppliers well – The process would have been that much harder if we had selected suppliers that had not been as incredibly supportive as the ones we used. This requires doing good research up front, looking off the beaten track, and also using social media like Twitter can put you in contact with amazing ideas and suppliers that you may not have found otherwise.

Accept that the wedding you have in your head at the beginning will not be the one that happens on the day. This is a good thing. By accepting that things change, and adapting your expectations and ideas along the way, I guarantee that you will have the wedding that is right for you both. That way, on the day you can sit back, let it happen and really enjoy the occasion.

A word for the lady; come on, say something emotional about your bride...

She's my conscience and my compass in life, and I cannot image life without her; she is everything to me. While she may have looked a million dollars to everyone at the wedding, I don't think she realises that she looks that way to me every day.

Five things every
father of the bride should know

1
This is going to get emotional

Despite what the Steve Martin (or Spencer Tracy if we're really going back) film Father of the Bride would have us believe, being the father of the bride is not all dealing with foreign-sounding wedding planners and comedic misunderstandings. The father of the bride has one of the most emotional roles to play in the wedding party – you've got tears and tantrums coming up, and that's just from the groom on his stag do. Then you have to deal with walking your daughter down the aisle and the dreaded speech. Are you ready to deal with it? Start preparing here: **www.iamstaggered.com/ father-of-the-bride**

2
You might not be paying but you need to be planning

Our recent groom survey revealed that these days only 8% of fathers of the bride pay for the wedding. That's still nearly 1 in 10 though and if that's you, we salute you and suggest you take a look at our free budget planner. If you're not paying for the bash don't think you can, or should, leave the wedding planning to the women. Your daughter will be amazed if you've got useful suggestions for the planning which handily you can steal from this here publication.

3
Most dads fear the wedding ceremony

We did warn you it was going to be emotional and you don't get much more emotional than the final act of walking your daughter down the aisle before handing her over to another man. We polled 100 dads on what they'd discussed with their daughters before this momentous occasion, read their thoughts at **www.bit.ly/ atCcpH** As for the long walk – just take it one step at a time and you'll be fine.

4

You need to look your best

All eyes will be on you as the proud father of the bride and that means that you will want to look your best. Our advice is that you should get involved early on in the discussions about what the groom is wearing, because the chances are you'll end up wearing the same.

5

Your speech shouldn't just thank people for coming

Our article on writing your speech is going to help you plan out exactly what you want to say on this once-in-a-lifetime (depending on daughter numbers) occasion. When you think about it, it's really pretty rare in modern life that we stop to listen to one another and that just makes this opportunity all the more important. You've got this golden chance to tell an assembled collection of friends, relatives and your loved ones exactly how you feel – make the most of it and don't worry if it gets emotional – that's what being a father of the bride is all about.

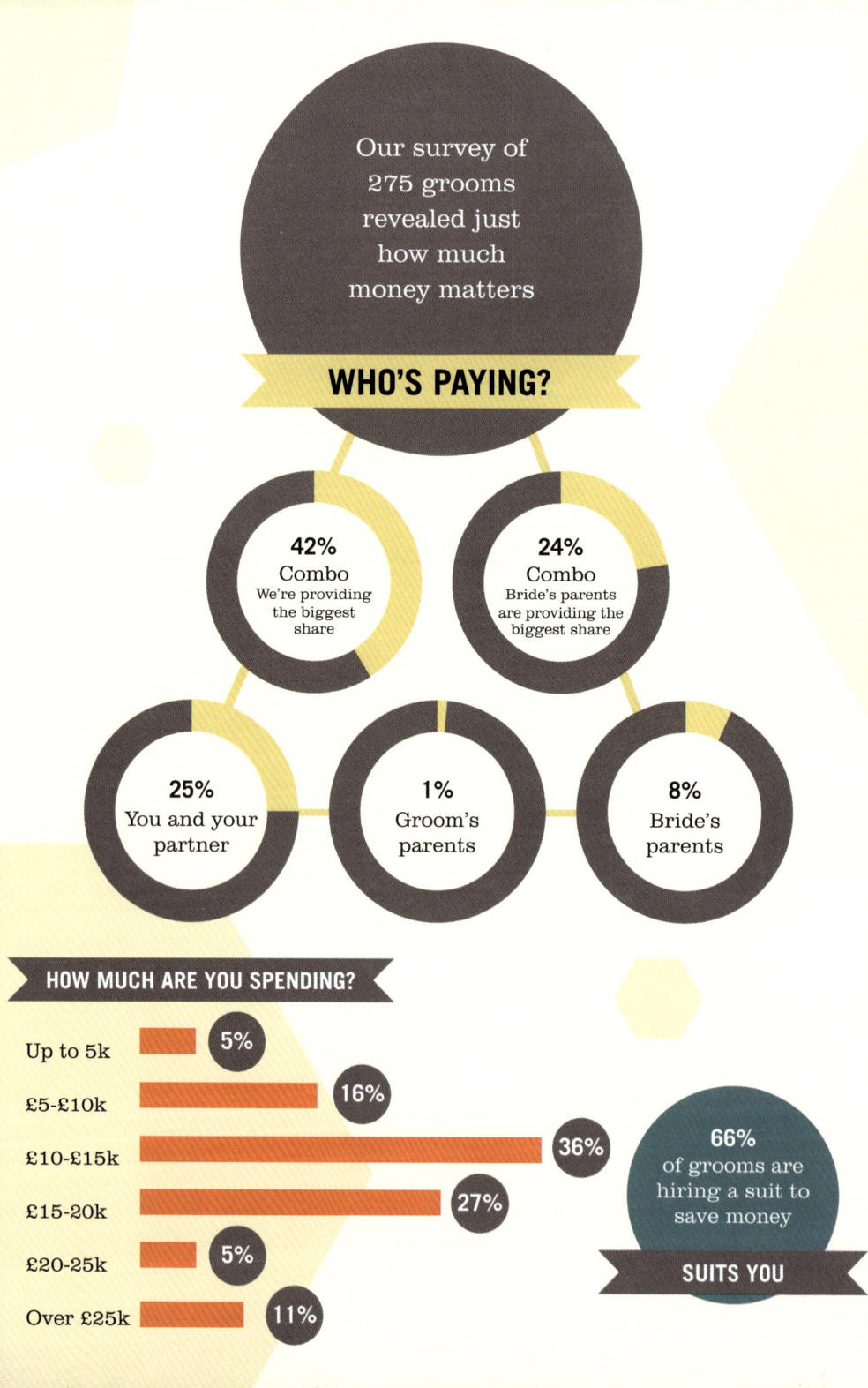

Our survey of 275 grooms revealed just how much money matters

WHO'S PAYING?

42%
Combo
We're providing the biggest share

24%
Combo
Bride's parents are providing the biggest share

25%
You and your partner

1%
Groom's parents

8%
Bride's parents

HOW MUCH ARE YOU SPENDING?

Up to 5k — 5%
£5-£10k — 16%
£10-£15k — 36%
£15-20k — 27%
£20-25k — 5%
Over £25k — 11%

66% of grooms are hiring a suit to save money

SUITS YOU

The A to Z of Wedding Planning
for Men

A - AMARYLLIS (THEY'RE FLOWERS)

Don't worry if you didn't know that the amaryllis was a flower, that was totally culled from Wikipedia. The thing to remember about flowers is that they probably represent the steepest learning curve for men and weddings, they can also cost a huge amount, but with an understanding florist you can find the right flowers.

The price of each flower varies. For example, carnations and chrysanthemums are relatively low cost, whilst peonies, orchids and old English roses are on the higher end of the scale. The cost of flowers, similar to holidays, rise for when people want them the most. A wedding venue booked in February may be lower cost, but buying flowers near Valentines' Day won't be.

The other big factor in calculating the cost of your flowers is volume. Do you want a bride's bouquet and two buttonholes, or are you filling a church and a marquee with flowers, along with bride's bouquet and six bridesmaids' bouquets?

For a smart approach consider alternatives to buttonholes but also choose flowers that need little extra adornment – orchids need little else to look good so volume is lower and likewise the costs. You could also consider using potted flowers such as hydrangeas, daisies and hyacinths which all work for the wedding especially as you can transfer them to your (or a relative's) garden afterwards. Alternatively, they work well as favours for guests.

B - BUDGET

One of the most critical aspects of your wedding and the sort of topic we could write an entire book about. The most salient points are these: forget average budgets, you'll hear anything from £15,000 to £25,000 but the only budget that counts is yours. It's reasonable for you to spend a good amount on celebrating your decision to get married, but if at any point you're risking your future happiness together by taking on too much debt then it's time to ask serious questions and start slashing the guest list.

Turn to P68

for the full lowdown on Jon Solomon's wedding as pictured here

C - CARS

We've seen every conceivable form of wedding transport ranging from Tuk Tuks, barges, London buses, Hackney Carriages and even tanks (**www.tanklimo.com**) but most people go with the conventional car and these are the top five.

1. Rolls-Royce Phantom

A stately legacy of the era when automobiles were so much more than just a means of getting from A to B, the legendary Phantom is the Daddy of wedding cars. It's a masterclass in opulence and not for the timid.
COST: Around £695 for 3 hours

2. 1940s Austin Princess

Don't be put off by the A-word – this dashing automobile is a world away from the spectacularly drab Allegro and Maestro.

3. Bentley Arnage

Only available for hire from a select few companies, the Arnage has a commanding presence and is perfect if you fancy something prestigious.
COST: Around £450 for 3 hours

4. Aston Martin

Winning wheels for the discerning man – guaranteed to add some 'wow factor' to your Big Day. And if your surname happens to be Bond, it's a no-brainer.
COST: Around £495+ for 3 hours

5. Beauford – 1930s Open Tourer

This vintage lovely re-captures a bygone era in unbeatable style, if you're yearning for a bit of retro.
COST: Around £450 for 3 hours

NORTON&
TOWNSEND

BESPOKE TAILORING

IT'S YOUR
WEDDING
TOO

Wear what you want.
Just make sure it fits.

Norton & Townsend
Bespoke wedding suits
from just £495

www.nortonandtownsend.co.uk

D - DATES

Dates to avoid 2012/2013. This could just as conceivably come under O for Olympics, given that the most hyped event across 2012 will be the Olympic games, hosted in London. For London weddings in the summer this is going to require a whole level of logistics planning because transport and facilities will be stretched to their upmost.

Things To Check Your Wedding Date Against:
- Bank holidays
- Sporting fixtures - http://bit.ly/ebILgZ
- Easter
- Unlucky dates – Friday the thirteenths and April Fools are obvious but also consider the impact of other dates too such as 7th July or 11th September
- Daylight saving days – Losing an hour's sleep isn't going to help your guests chance of getting to your wedding on time
- Saints' Days – For the patriots amongst you
- Christmas and New Year
- Music festivals - Full list of festivals **www.efestivals.co.uk/festivals**

E - ENTERTAINMENT

The rule with wedding entertainment is that it should fit the theme of the day and be something that you genuinely enjoy. It sounds stupid to even say that but so many people just assume that you need to have something like a first dance that they go along with it without even thinking if they actually want one.

Photobooths and Chinese Lanterns were the big news in 2011 and look to continue their popularity in 2012. However, we're tipping a return for the popularity of a fireworks display, a much underrated way of wrapping the night up.

DJs and bands remain the evening must have, but other forms of entertainment such as arguing waiters and close-up magicians have become a popular way for breaking the ice at the stage where guests are first sipping their on-arrival drink. Speak to your wedding planner or venue co-ordinator and keep your mind open.

F - FAVOURS

It's a toss-up between flowers and favours as to the men's least favourite aspect of the wedding planning. It's often because all of the little bits seem so unnecessary – sneak a look at her wedding magazines and you'll see them trying to convince her that she needs to buy a load of empty bird cages for the centre of the tables – madness!

Favours are a traditional thank-you gift for guests which give them something to go away with. You're probably thinking that feeding them and giving them some free drink is gift enough and we're on your side on this one. However, once you look past the sugared almonds (why!) there are some really good ideas for favours that represent the couple. Our top three:
- A mix CD containing some of the bride and groom's favourite music.
- Donating to charity - check out Oxfam Unwrapped and Cancer Research UK's schemes
- Writing in-jokes or filthy phrases on personalised Love Hearts or M&Ms.

G - GIFT LIST

The issue of gifts is one that is guaranteed to set the forums alight. The truth is that in previous generations the wedding was the point where the couple set up home together, these days we're all living in sin from the second we get together with our partners, and as a result we have all the pots and pans we need. It's still a nice opportunity to get matching plates and cutlery sets but you can see why more and more couples are opting for something a bit more fun.

Unfortunately, there's nothing that gets guests' (especially English guests) backs up more than being asked to give money. There are alternatives though. We've seen a number of gift lists appearing for art, honeymoons (Buy Our Honeymoon) and even music. It's your decision but it's worth appreciating that with the cost of attending a wedding hitting an all-time high (over £300 on average), that extra request for money to build your conservatory might just grate on your much-loved guests' nerves. At least invite them to come and see it when it's done.

H - HOG ROAST

We polled our readers for the "classic" wedding meals they were bored of eating. Here's the top five:
- Soup, or ham and melon starter
- Chicken wrapped in prosciutto/Parma ham/bacon
- Goat's cheese tart
- Dried out roast beef
- Whole poached salmon

The Staggered Office's List of Foods You Never Get Tired of Eating:
- Roast lamb
- Bacon sandwiches (especially baps, especially in the evening), but lots of extra ketchup please, no sachets.
- Curry at 10pm
- Hog roast
- Fish and chips
- Cheese and biscuits (especially with a drop of port)

I - INVITATIONS

There is an unbelievable amount of companies doing wedding stationery these days. This gives couples a huge amount to choose from – take a look at the suppliers list at the end of The Staggered Groom Guide and check out various examples on the site. The other big development is the number of kits that allow you to do it yourself, again lots of examples on the site.

However, it's not just the artefact of the invitation that you need to consider, it's the question of who to invite. It's arguable that between this and the seating plan is where most of the arguments occur. Keep your head. There will be lots of discussions around "You have to have Uncle X" and it's up to you to draw the line where you and your budget are comfortable. You will consider eloping several times. You can always separate guests by day (who you generally bung a meal and some drink at) and the evening crowd (who you might give a drink and a bacon bap to). Needless to say, tweaking who is on what list allows you to massively change the budget. If you need an excuse pick a venue where numbers are naturally restricted, a lift for example.

Turn to P98
to find out who forgot the bridal gift

PHOTOGRAPH: BECKY AND NEIL BUTTERWORTH

J - JEWELLERY

There's lots of jewellery associated with weddings, and you'll probably not be surprised to find that you'll be responsible for buying much of it. However, this is about one specific piece of jewellery – the bridal gift. We're always a little bit terrified by how many grooms don't realise that they're supposed to give the bride a gift on the wedding day. It doesn't matter that you've just spent thousands of pounds creating her dream wedding day, if you forget to buy her a gift you'll hear about it for the rest of your life.

Jewellery is obviously one option, and if you're quick you can reserve one of the "something old, something new, something borrowed, something blue" categories that the bride has to wear and theme your bride gift around that. Other options are flowers, perfume, underwear or something entirely personal - good luck with that!

A classy touch is to have the gift delivered on the wedding day along with a letter you've written to her. It doesn't have to be full of sonnets, but something that tells her how you feel will get you bonus points. Try not to rely on Royal Mail but it might be something that an usher or best man could be despatched to do while you get ready.

K - KRAPPY KUFFLINKS

When it comes to buying a gift for your ushers and best man to thank them for representing you on the day, please can we all agree that cufflinks and socks with the words "best man" or "usher" on them are not an appropriate way to sum up your love and admiration for these most important of men. Our favourite gift suggestion is to buy them tickets for any event you care to go to – gig, sporting event, festival. The best ones are if they're a month or two after the wedding. This is a good idea for three reasons 1) you get to go as well 2) it gives you something to look forward to after the wedding 3) it tells your friends (and your wife-to-be) that your friendship with these guys will persist after the wedding – it won't be a case of you never seeing them again. As a bonus you can also maybe get it paid for out of the wedding budget.

Real Groom

Phil Wong

Age: 30
The Bride: Ann
The Best Man: My younger brother Anthony

What can you tell us about your stag do?
A weekend in Swansea with 15 lads, canoeing, canyoning and drinking! No stories... but just like to say that canyoning is very dangerous, especially with a hangover! The highlight was jumping off a 20ft waterfall.

Where did you get married?
Moxhull Hall for our outdoor ceremony, China Court Restaurant for the reception and then Moxhull Hall again for the after party and BBQ

What did the men wear on the day?
I wore two different suits on the day, a grey two-buttoned lounge suit and a tux to complement Ann's dress changes. Both suits were tailor made by Masky in Hong Kong as I find it quite difficult to find a good fit off the rails.

With my tux I wore a red mini chequered shirt from Crombie with a skinny bow tie and braces and then changed into a classic tux shirt later in the day. For my main look, I wore the grey lounge suit with an ivory waistcoat, the shirt and tie bar were from TM Lewin and cufflinks and tie bar from Agnes B.

My groomsmen all wore their own grey suits and we provided the stripey grey/silver ties and we all had white pocket squares as a finishing touch.

What advice would you give to future grooms?
Don't panic- make your boys do your work but make sure they know what they need to do – military style! Have fun and enjoy the day. Don't get carried away with spending – it can get so out of hand! Devise a budget and stick to it!

A word for the lady...
They say you know you're having fun when time passes quickly... I must be having fun, as it's been five months since our wedding and seven years since we got together and time has whizzed by. Can't wait to have more fun!

L - LOVE

We've said this a few times through The Staggered Groom Guide – weddings and marriages are about love. You'll probably be the more sensible of the two of you (that's not meant to sound sexist, women just tend to get a bit, um, deranged around weddings) so it's for you to keep remembering this point. The wedding is going to be one of the best days of your life, but only because it means that from that day forward you get to spend every day with the woman you love. One of the most essential tools you'll need for wedding planning is a sense of perspective and that comes from remembering about Love.

M - MOTHER IN LAW

An anagram for Mother in law is "woman hitler". Just saying. If you're experiencing an overly-involved mother-in-law (or any other source of unasked for advice), here's how to deal with it:

- **Present A United Front** Discuss with your wife-to-be why you feel like you're being pushed out and get her to understand how it's making you feel. Try to explain why you want your views to be heard and for the wedding to be a joint adventure.

- **Be Tactful** You don't even have to bring up the fact that you're feeling like your M-I-L is becoming too dominant. You can simply explain to her that you're very thankful for all of her help and that you have a particular set of tasks that you'd like her input on. Explain you're covering tasks A-to-W and you'd love it if she could take care of Y and Z.

- **Don't be threatened financially** If she's wielding the power because her husband is paying you may need to ask if the cost of her involvement is higher than you're willing to pay.

N - NERVES

Cold feet, wedding jitters, depression as a result of financial pressures, fear of being the centre of attention. Only some of this is acceptable. If you are starting to get worried, anxious or outright depressed by the wedding then you need help. It might just be that you need a night to talk it over with a friend, or you could require a full on intervention. Either way, do not delay in getting help. Start here: **www.iamstaggered. com/wedding-nerves**

O - OFF THE RACK

This is a suit question. The point being do you want to wear a suit you buy, or a suit you hire. And if you want to buy it do you want to go to a shop and buy it off the rack or go to a tailor and have it made. These are effectively your three choices and there are merits to all of them.

Hiring means you can wear something more traditional (think tails, frock coats) as it's unlikely you'd want to buy something like that to wear it again. It also means you can hire in bulk and have all of the grooms party looking the same (or similar).

Based on our latest reader's survey the ratio is around 66% hire and 34% buy. This seems to be a growing trend. The reason being that a) lots of men don't particularly like tails b) if you're paying approximately £100 to hire a suit for one day, why not spend £250 and have a suit made to measure? This is especially true when you consider the bride is spending thousands (probably) on a dress she'll only wear once.

It's your call – we have plenty of options in our Suppliers section for hiring or buying but make your own choice and stick to it. Plenty of mothers-in-law won't like the lounge suit option but if it's what makes you feel good it's the right answer.

P - PHOTOGRAPHERS AND VIDEOGRAPHERS

This can be one of the best bits of the wedding, it's certainly the historical record you'll enjoy for generations to come. Set your budget and stick to it, but this is one area where we advise going big. Yes, everyone knows someone who has a fancy camera who says they can do them, but this is how you'll remember the day, is that what you want? We are also overwhelmingly in favour of videographers. Everyone we know who uses one says that they watch the video more than look at the photos – they're generally cheaper too.

There are different styles of photographer from the formal to the documentary, to the experimental. Take a look at their sites but also remember to meet them in person and see if you actually enjoy their company. Think about doing an engagement shoot to try them out (many photographers offer this as part of a package) and don't be afraid to ask for the photos you want. It's also a good idea to make a list of all the group shots you would like and make sure the photographer has a copy.

Q - QUOTATIONS

Amazing how useful it is to have a few quotations about love, whether it's for the guestbook or for your letter to your wife, slip one of these bad boys in and you're all good. Please note: do not quote Bad Boys.

"For you see, marriage is a lot like an orange. First, you have the skin... then the sweet, sweet innards..."
Homer Simpson

"Marriage is like a tense, unfunny version of Everybody Loves Raymond, only it doesn't last 22 minutes. It lasts forever."
Paul Rudd, Knocked Up

"Who, being loved, is poor?"
Oscar Wilde

"Now Join your Hands. And with your Hands, your Hearts."
William Shakespeare

"Men are from Earth. Women are from Earth. Deal with it."
George Carlin

"When you realize you want to spend the rest of your life with somebody, you want the rest of your life to start as soon as possible."
When Harry Met Sally

R - RINGS

You've probably already bought the engagement rings (have a look at www.iamstaggered.com/getting-engaged if not) but the wedding rings sorted. There's so much choice these days that it's worth speaking to a specialist jeweller who can take you through all the options. If you want to get an idea of costs for a bespoke, original ring fill in the form at **www.iamstaggered.com/getting-engaged/design-your-own-rings** and our jewellery specialist will get in touch and advise for free. The big trend we're predicting for 2012 is a continued demand for bespoke rings using pieces of jewellery from family members.

S - SERVICE

The ceremony of the wedding – either a church service or a registry office service is the central point of the day. It's also something that a lot of grooms get a bit nervous about. The trick to make it more comfortable is to get involved in the planning of the ceremony. If there are elements you're looking forward to, songs you'll enjoy and so on then it's a lot less pressure.

In actual fact the whole service is often incredibly joyful, rather than nerve-wracking (but check out **www.iamstaggered.com/wedding-ceremony** for some more in-depth advice). You'll want to pick readings, hymns (or songs), entry and exit music. Then you'll want to have a think about what sort of ceremony you want. These vary massively from Greek Orthodox (about fifteen hours) to humanist (short, secular and sweet) to the perfunctory legal service. Make your choices and look forward to it. Just don't write "help me" on your shoes – it's been done.

T – TAKE HER TO SOME WEDDING FAIRS

Staggered does a lot of wedding fairs per year and for men they're sometimes infuriating, sometimes useful. They're infuriating because there'll be nothing there for you (unless we're there of course) and you'll be largely ignored by the wedding suppliers. Damn it all though, they're useful. The reason they're useful is because they condense about 15 weekends' worth of traipsing around the shops into one exhausting day. Our tip: bring a trolley and some stickers with your personal details (including name, email address and wedding date). You'll get so many brochures thrown at you and speak to so many photographers, but you'll probably tick three or four things off your "to do list" and get a much better sense of what you do and don't like. File under "grin and bear it."

U – USHERS

The forgotten men of the wedding. They're usually good friends, or close family who you want to be involved but not quite the positions for your best men. There's significant debate on the Staggered forums about whether having two best men is a cop-out and if you should pick one. It seems to be a rising trend though, so don't feel guilty about stretching the definition of "best man". It's your call, but don't overlook how useful your ushers can be. Give them clearly defined jobs to do and they'll help make your day perfect.

V – VENUES

One of the first things you'll have to choose is the venue. Often with wedding venues putting together packages it also means that by choosing your venue it sorts the food, cake and sometimes even the honeymoon. It should go without saying but shop around. Be picky. Explain your precise requirements. Even if a venue holds hundreds of weddings each year, this is the only one you'll ever have and you want it to be uniquely about you.

W – WEDDING INSURANCE

Get it. Go to **compareweddinginsurance.org.uk** choose your package and get it. For the relatively small cost you can ensure that if anything goes wrong, you'll not be left without some backup. Get it.

X – YOU MAY KISS THE BRIDE

This shouldn't be too arduous but along with the other aspects of the service, you'll want to practice your first kiss, it's arguably the defining moment of the marriage ceremony so you should make sure that you don't go for the full on tongues and wandering hands while your wife (because that's what she now is) opts for the relatives-friendly peck.

Y – YOUR NEW BEST FRIEND

We're all for making the wedding easier for you, that's why we think you should give serious help to hiring a wedding planner. Yes, you're probably thinking that it's an extra expense that you can do without but consider this: wedding planners are professionals who create great weddings every single day. This means that they know all the suppliers, they know the venues, they have seen every single problem you're likely to encounter. The vast majority of them are bloody good at their jobs (if you want to avoid a dud always check they're a member of UKAWP). Whatever you pay for their services you'll almost certainly make back in discounts from suppliers and you'll have the benefit of their support and wisdom on the day.

Z – ZIPS

You're going to spend a lot of time making sure you look good on your wedding day, but there are some fatally obvious mistakes you can make to ruin your look, brief your best man on these and keep checking thoughout the day:
- Zips up
- Food in teeth
- Ties straight
- Phones and keys making an unsightly bulge in your pocket
- Sweat patches, choose industrial strength anti-perspirant and dark shirts if you're worried about looming sweat patches

Turn to P92
to find out in which order
you should kiss the bride
and drink your lager

Greyeye Photography, cool a

www.greyeyephoto.com

On your marks
It's not a sprint, it's a
marathon - and then
a sprint

What you have to do

and when you have to do it

Congratulations, you're involved with a wedding! That means whether you
know it or not your To Do List just became really, really full. Whether you're
a groom, best man or father of the bride, there's a whole list of things you'll
need to do to ensure the smooth running of the big day. The only blind spot
is what these things are and when you're expected to do them. Panic not
though, because this wedding planner countdown for blokes will guide you
through the next chapter in your lives.

: PRE-ENGAGEMENT

G Work out if you're going to be all traditional and ask for her father's permission. Seal that deal, work out what engagement ring to buy (or pick a nice placeholder ring) and then book the engagement weekend.

G Get the all-important "yes". Without that there's not much we can do to help...

12 : MONTHS

G B F Join Staggered (**www.iamstaggered.com/ wp-signup.php**) – it'll keep you up-to-date with everything you need to know, give you loads of ideas to get brownie points and maybe even win you some swag.

G B If you're thinking of having an engagement party and haven't yet, now's the time. It's another great excuse for a celebration, so why not? It's also a good chance to get material for the speech and practice what it'll be like to make your wedding speech by making a toast.

G F Work out who's going to be paying for the wedding and how much you've got to spend. If the pot's looking a little empty, work out how you can boost the fund. If you need to save up, work out how long it will take as this might impact on the wedding date. And if you're going cap-in-hand to parents and future parents-in-law, do spend some time buttering them up first.

G Work out a realistic wedding budget incorporating all the necessary purchases, from venue to dress and everything in between. Research prices online, but the bottom line is that everything's going to cost more than you think – welcome to the Wedding Industry.

G Think about attending a wedding fair. It's not going to be as much fun as a day at Alton Towers, but you might pick up some ideas.

G Feign interest in the wedding magazines you're being shown. If you're after brownie points get a subscription for your Mrs-to-be.

G If you're thinking of hiring a wedding planner (and you should because the good ones will save you hassle and money), now's the time to get them involved in order to take maximum advantage of their services. Check they're a member of **www.ukawp.com** before hiring them.

G Start a wedding file to keep all wedding-related documents and contracts in. It might just help you stay sane further down the line.

G **F** Decide how many guests you'd like and work out a rough guest list. Ask the families if there are any people they'd like you to invite.

G If you're planning a church wedding, book your chosen church as early as possible. If you aren't regular churchgoers but want to marry in a church, you may need to become considerably more religious – so cancel your Sunday morning footie engagements for the foreseeable. If you're going for a non-churchy wedding, start looking into possible venues, and consider doing the service and reception in the same place.

G Book reception venue and caterers. Check the cancellation/refund policies before stumping up the cash, and make sure you have the policies in writing. If you're spending a lot on the day then think about getting wedding insurance in place that will cover you if anyone's ill or, um, jilted.

G When you've decided on the where, work out the when. More than likely it's the availability of your venue and/or church that will decide the wedding date, but do remember that some dates are better than others, so check our A to Z planner to help miss the important dates. Be realistic and give yourself enough time to plan the wedding properly – a glance down this list should remind you just how much work you have to do. When you're sure of the details, send out 'save the date' cards (or a Save The Date video if you're being all new media about things) to the guests you definitely want to see at the ceremony.

G Book entertainment for the reception if you're having any. If you're going for a DJ, go by personal recommendation where possible.

G Name the best man and ushers and enjoy a guilt-free celebratory booze-up. Do NOT throw this opportunity away lightly, make your wife-to-be understand that this is emotional man stuff and you want to do this right and make a weekend of it. You've proposed, now it's time to bropose.

G **B** **F** ...But don't hit the sauce too hard – you need to start getting in shape now unless you want to look like the Pilsbury Dough Boy in a suit.

09 : MONTHS

G You've got the basics now the finer details are being put in place. If you're set on marrying in Elvis Jumpsuits, now's the time to pipe up and wait for the horrified response. Incidentally, if you're already finding yourself faced with a Bridezilla situation then you need to start putting your foot down now before the wedding gets out of control.

G Book the wedding cars.

G Book photographer and/or videographer.

B Start thinking about the stag weekend. Remember to plan big. Go for the stag do classics by all means but originality is always welcomed and that needs an extra bit of planning.

G Order the cake and flowers, book hotel rooms for the wedding and start planning your honeymoon. Remember to tell the boss you'll need time off.

G Buy the wedding rings.

06 : MONTHS

G **B** **F** Buy suits or arrange wedding suit hire for the best man and ushers. Have the discussion about whether you can pull off a top hat or not and then discuss your other style accessory options

G Order the wedding invitations and stationery.

G Finalise details with the venue and confirm the menu and catering details with the caterer. Check, check and double-check.

B Understand that your mate has gone into the wedding planning underworld where his life consists of looking at swatches of material and wondering what on earth he's supposed to be picking out. Take him for a weekly night out to take his mind off things, then fill him full of beer and take the blame from his Mrs.

G Set up your wedding list. Contemplate whether you really can put an X-Box on there among the matching towels. Remember to include items to suit all budgets. Don't think you have to go with a department store there are loads of great options for gift lists now – everything from Not On The High Street, Amazon Wishlists and Buy Our Honeymoon.

G Buy bitty bits like wedding favours if you're having them, and a wedding book for guests to sign.

G Choose music, readings and vows for the ceremony.

G Honeymoon decision time. Are you booking it together, or are you surprising her? Either way you need to get it booked and start working out how to pay for it. Don't forget honeymoons are all about the details and little surprises, so get planning about how to make it extra special.

G Meet and confirm details with the minister or registrar.

B Finalise plans for the stag do. Don't tell the bride. While you think of it though – email her to ask for any ideas/material that she may have to add into your speech.

B Start an email list/private Facebook group to keep all the stags in regular contact before the day.

G Consider any elements you might have forgotten, like glassware for the reception.

G **B** **F** Discuss moving the speeches to the beginning of the wedding breakfast, or even to the beginning of the day if you're feeling really nervous about the speeches. Yes, it's tradition to do it after the meal – but what's the point of paying £30 for some food you're not going to be able to enjoy?

G Send out wedding invitations. A Facebook event invite will not suffice. Remember to include maps, directions, chosen local hotels/B+Bs to the ceremony and reception.

B Sort out the stag do t-shirts. Book them early to get the best price. Make any final arrangements for the stag do. Keep on top of the stragglers.

01 : MONTH

G Buy presents for the best man and ushers, bridesmaids and parents. DO NOT FORGET TO BUY THE BRIDE A GIFT. It sounds crazy but it's tradition and you'll get skinned if you forget.

B If you haven't had the stag do yet, now's the time. The next fortnight is going to be manic. Be extra smooth and book the groom something to help him recover. Even if it's just a pack of Rennie wrapped in a bow. Use the stag do as a chance to get stories about the groom off all the people who know him.

B Follow up the stag do by circulating any good pictures through the email list or Facebook group. The aim is to keep people in touch so they remember each other again by the wedding.

G **B** **F** Write wedding speeches.

G Chase any late RSVPs and think about the seating plan. Once done, advise caterers or the reception venue of final numbers.

02 : WEEKS

B Distribute order of service sheets.

B Organise a contact list for the wedding with all the numbers you'll need (ushers, reception, vicar and so on). That way you can sort out any issues on the day.

G Finalise seating plan and write place cards.

01 : WEEK

G **B** **F** Get yourselves shipshape. Have haircuts, get a back, sack and crack wax and attack the mono-brow with tweezers. WARNING: Don't do anything drastic without letting her know you're going for a Mr T.

G Pack for your honeymoon.

B Pick up any hired outfits.

G **B** **F** Wear in your wedding shoes so you don't end the day with corns. Some dress shoes have polished soles, which do not go well with stone church floors. Get a cobbler to set a strip of rubber on the sole if you're worried about it affecting your dance moves/aisle-walking abilities.

01 : DAY

B Check all is in order with the suits. Offer to return them for the groom and ushers – he's going to have enough on his mind and it's another thing off his to do list.

G Give the best man a list of duties for the day, plus cash to pay suppliers and several warnings about remembering the rings.

B DON'T lose the rings. Don't even PRETEND to lose the rings.

G **B** **F** Get a good night's sleep. Or at least intend to.

00 : WEDDING DAY

G **B** **F** Check the reception venue as early as possible to make sure there are no disasters. Don't forget to dispatch an usher with any gifts so they are all at the reception and ready to go.

G **B** **F** Eat breakfast, and beware early boozing.

F Have some words of wisdom and love ready for your daughter and enjoy the walk down the aisle.

G Look at her as she's coming down the aisle. Try not to cry. Say 'I do' and 'I will' in all the right places.

G **B** **F** Stand up. Give Speeches. Enjoy applause.

G **B** **F** Relax. You've earned it.

The big day
When the ceremony comes just try to relax and enjoy it. See page 94

PHOTOGRAPH: GREENFIELD PHOTOGRAPHY

: POST WEDDING

G Set up a recurring event in your calendar to nudge you about anniversary gifts.

B **F** Don't forget to send a card on the anniversary.

Real Groom
Bean

Age: 29
Bride's Name: Anna
Best Man: Hunter

Where was your stag do – any scars?
Started off with a cut-throat shave at a traditional barbers, then after lunch off to a Turkish bathhouse (the idea of a friend who handily didn't turn up as he was off travelling in Asia) where I was subjected to a vigorous massage by a small, middle-aged Turkish man before a sauna, steam room and plunge pool.

Despite dragging me to a sports shop to buy a pair of trunks, Hunter managed to forget his own and as the place was "clothing optional" (and men only) he sufficed with only a towel – apart from for the plunge pool which was, of course, freezing and so not the most flattering occasion to be naked in front of your friends. After that it was back to the hotel to get suited up for an evening of steaks, booze and naked ladies. Nothing too "crazy" and everybody had a great time without any real incident, which part of me thinks is a little disappointing, the rest of me is relieved.

What did you wear?
My outfit was a bespoke Dashing Tweed suit tailored by Graham Browne, a made to measure shirt from Stephan Haroutunian, velvet braces by Albert Thurston, a pair of burgundy suede brogues from Russell & Bromley and the tie was from Austin Reed.

What three pieces of advice would you give to other blokes going through the whole wedding thing now?
1. You'll not have enough time to keep track, so make sure you've got at least one or two out of your best man/ ushers/bridesmaids who you can trust to make sure everything goes vaguely according to plan.

2. That said, it's pretty likely a few things won't, so don't worry too much and certainly don't let any sort of negativity get you down. As long as you get married, the food turns up and everyone has a good time then everything else is a bonus.

3. Make sure your tie is done up properly and check it every so often. I didn't and I can see it in every single photo and it annoys the hell out of me. And don't fiddle with your hair when you're nervous.

Claim Your **FREE** Staggered Budget Planner

There's no escaping it: if you want to keep a handle on your wedding finances then you're going to have to get pretty comfy with Excel. Unfortunately, Microsoft's legendary spreadsheet software is about as easy to pick up as a jellied eel in a pool full of Fairy liquid.

For that reason we've put Staggered team member Dan Woodward (himself a Real Groom – check him out on P14) to work. Dan is a black belt in Excel and has created a budget planner that keeps track of your money, calculates the remaining payments and gives you an overview of your finances.

If that weren't enough, it's also got a guest tracker so you can keep a close tab on who is coming to the wedding and any arrangements that need to be made. In short, it's a piece of genius, and we've seen similar software for sale around for £50, so we think it makes for a pretty nice readers' gift. If you have any questions, problems or suggestions then please feel free to get in touch **0844 310 4050** or **info@iamstaggered.com**

To claim your free staggered budget planner

- Join Staggered (if you haven't already) – it's free and takes less than a minute: **www.iamstaggered.com/wp-signup.php**
- Visit - **www.iamstaggered.com/free-staggered-budget-planner**
- Enter the password "**money**" and follow the instructions on the page.

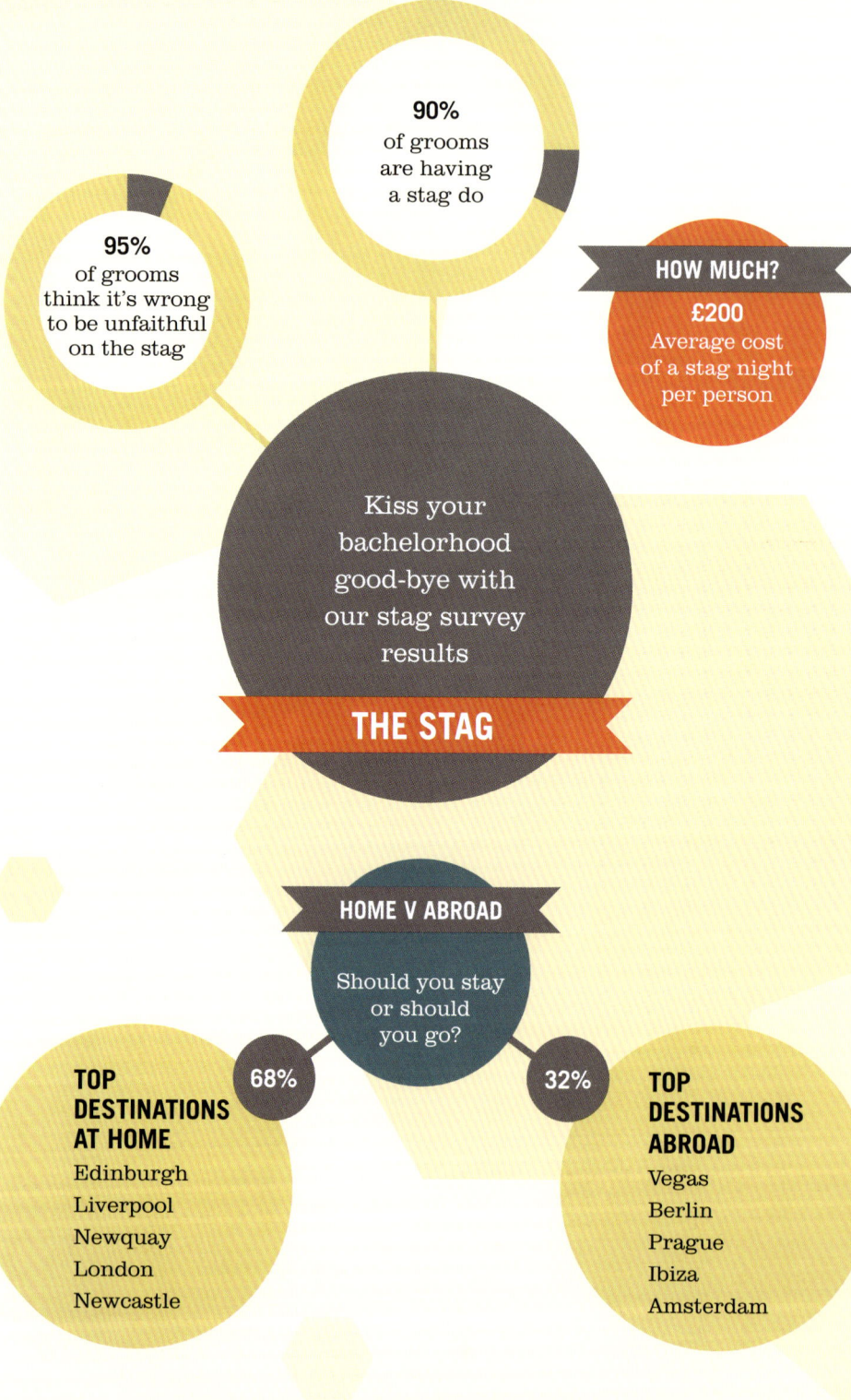

90%
of grooms
are having
a stag do

95%
of grooms
think it's wrong
to be unfaithful
on the stag

HOW MUCH?
£200
Average cost
of a stag night
per person

Kiss your
bachelorhood
good-bye with
our stag survey
results

THE STAG

HOME V ABROAD

Should you stay
or should
you go?

68%

32%

**TOP
DESTINATIONS
AT HOME**
Edinburgh
Liverpool
Newquay
London
Newcastle

**TOP
DESTINATIONS
ABROAD**
Vegas
Berlin
Prague
Ibiza
Amsterdam

Sorting the Stag

Best man, eh? Been given the responsibility but fairly sure that you can't organise a booze-up in a brewery? Don't worry – stag nights might take some serious planning, but it's all stuff you can do in manageable chunks. Follow this simple guide and you can't go far wrong.

BEFORE THE EVENT

Talk to the stag

Just as every little girl has a perfect wedding in mind, so every young boy sketches out their dream stag night long before they pop the question. Ask the stag what he wants from his, be it a weekend away, an adventure day and a booze-up or a quiet night in the local. It's much easier to work from a brief. And do remember that it's not your stag night you're planning – it's all for your good buddy's benefit. If you're researching ideas head to www.iamstaggered.com/book-your-stag-do/ and make use of our experience in this field, you just take the credit.

Make a guest list

Ask the groom-to-be to think about which friends he'd like to see at the stag do and work out a list of between eight and 20 key people. Try and keep it to proper friends and shave off the acquaintances and work mates – more than 20 is an unwieldy number to deal with. Any more and the groom often ceases to be the focus of attention.

Think hard about whether the bride's father, brother, etc should be in attendance as it may change the dynamic of the group – you can always arrange a separate affair for family. On this issue a lot depends on how you and the groom think the various friend circles will link up. Once again, working with the groom will help to identify any problem areas.

Make contact with the stags

Get the final list of names, numbers and email addresses from the groom and touch base with your charges. Group emails or a private Facebook group will be the easiest and least time-consuming way of keeping them in the loop. When you make contact, ask about their budget and if any of them have any special requirements – special diets, disabilities etc – that you might have to work around.

Look into the options

With the stag's opinions on board and an idea of the budgetary constraints of the guests, hit the net and look into the options. Obviously, if it's stag do ideas you're after then you'll want to head to www.iamstaggered.com/stag-do. If you've decided on a city break, think of the big European party cities like Barcelona, Berlin and Amsterdam (our stag do city guides – www.iamstaggered.com/stag-do-city-guides will help here).

If you want an activity weekend, look into paintballing, go-karting and outward bound centres. Think of some quirky alternatives too, and make the final, informed decision with the groom. If you're going with a stag operator be careful who you book with – some firms are better than others and a quick post on the forum is a good way of getting advice and ideas.

Hmm...
How do I drink beer in this thing?

Decide on a date

A stag do should be close to the wedding but not so close that it impacts on the main event – it's now universally agreed that stag dos the night before the wedding are a terrible idea. Come up with a few dates between two and five weeks before the big day, pitch them to the group and see which weekend is the least conflicted. Do this at least three to five months before the big day to prevent clashes in peoples' diaries.

Beware the passing of time

If you're planning a foreign trip, the best prices will be available early. Late deals aren't what they once were, and it's a risky strategy to leave it to the last minute if there's a big group of you. Rooms in hostels are good, cheap accommodation for stags, but again, are likely to book up early.

Name a treasurer

It's a good idea to set up a fund to pay for stag-related activities. It's likely there'll be one person in the group who's good with money, so play to his ego and appoint him as treasurer. Bingo! That's one thankless task off your hands. The treasurer needs to keep track of who's paid what and any expenditure. Importantly, they also need to chase the late payers (there will be several).

Don't be a nanny

Looking after a large group is a pain in the nethers, so farm out as much responsibility as possible. They're all grown men, but you'll be stunned at how many of them forget passports, don't bring their own trousers, etc. To avoid being the one responsible for nagging them all give out roles among the group (e.g. you're responsible for t-shirts, you're responsible for trouser reminders, etc)

Pranks and strippers

If you're going to pull a prank on the groom, make it a good one and tell Staggered about it afterwards. Plan it behind his back with the other party-goers to ensure success. If you're hiring a stripper, remember to phone the venue to check whether they'll allow her/him/them to do her/his/their stuff on the premises.

The key to a good stag prank is to make it personal – don't just go for the generic stag do pranks but think about the annoying habits of the groom and base it around that. For stag do pranks the bottom line is NO PERMANENT SCARRING – and that applies to physical and mental scarring.

Think about the dress code

It's common for stags to mark themselves out with some kind of themed dress code. Whether you're going for matching T-shirts or Ghostbusters costumes, some planning will be required. Do remember that matching

PHOTOGRAPH BELOW: DAVID MUSCROFT

clothes mark you out instantly as a stag party, which may make it tricky to get in certain places. And on a related note, if you're planning to hit venues that insist on shoes, make sure that everyone in the party knows and dresses accordingly.

Fill your faces

Don't forget that you will need to eat at some point, so book a restaurant in advance to make sure everyone gets a good bit of grub in. Your liver will love you for it.

Plan your venues

Bouncers can spot stag parties a mile off and, believe it or not, many pubs, clubs and bars don't relish the idea of a large bunch of smashed guys invading their establishment. Firstly, you're likely to be a little excitable. Secondly, you'll turn the place into a sausage-fest. To avoid being bratwurst-blocked at the door, book tables at a few chosen venues. They'll be expecting you, you should get some good service and you'll definitely get in.

Don't forget that although the number of venues you can legitimately get into as a stag party is reduced, you've got great bargaining power because you're potentially going to fill a venue up and drink a shedload of booze. ALWAYS ASK FOR GROUP DISCOUNTS AND SPECIAL OFFERS. Do it with a smile on your face and you'll be amazed what you can get offered.

DURING THE EVENT

Be authoritative

On the stag do itself, your role is that of a sheepdog, and you'll be expected to take charge and herd people from one location or activity to another. Even if this goes against the grain of your personality, you're the one who knows where you're supposed to be and when, so raise your voice and be heard. You should factor in some natural wastage of about two or three people per new places, so make sure everyone has contact numbers and an idea of where you're going so you can rendezvous.

Have a kitty

It stops people wandering off on their own or wriggling out of rounds.

Have some surprises up your sleeve

If the party is lagging – or even if it's not – it's a good idea to have some surprises for the groom and other stags, whether it's a limo, a stripper or something simple like hilarious old photos of the groom.

Be responsible

You may be planning some pranks for the groom on his big night, but remember that, ultimately, you want him to get home in one piece. Or maybe you want him to get home wearing a one-piece. Either way, he'll thank you for stepping in if the fun goes too far.

A Modern Groom

It's arguably the most important style day of your life. You want to look good, but above all, you want to look like you. We've discussed this at length with a number of brides who see the groom as little more than an accessory. Yes, you want to make your wife-to-be happy but that doesn't mean you have to dress like you've just stepped out of a Dickens' novel.

The modern groom dares to be himself...

PHOTOGRAPHY: SARAH GAWLER

Venue: Nonsuch Mansion. Clothes & Accessories: A Suit That Fits, Beyond Retro, Savvy Row – Vintage British Classics, Hunky Dory Vintage. Buttonholes: Vayle Spring Flowers. Hair and Makeup: Adjhani Barton. Model & Styling: Kev Soar

What to wear:
The basic options

The usual clothing associated with men and weddings is hugely formal, and if we're being honest, somewhat antiquated. Take a look at the Real Grooms featured through The Staggered Groom Guide and you'll see that more and more are opting for lounge suits or more modern three piece suits. Often this opens up the potential to buy the suit outright and wear it again, however, you might be champing at the bit to slip into something more formal. In which case it's important you know your Prince Edwards from your Prince Alberts (no, really). Read on.

Tailcoat

There are two variations on the tailcoat – the morning, and the evening. There's one big difference between the two, and that's buttons. Whereas the morning coat has one or two simple buttons holding the sweep of material together, the evening dress version has a series of buttons and is cut flush to the waist. The tailcoat options are not ideal for fat blokes because the way the jackets fall tends to expose the stomach area and if you're sporting a paunch, these will highlight the fact. You could reasonably expect to wear a top hat with either and waistcoats are obligatory with both looks. Canes and learning the Fred Astaire dance moves are optional.

Prince Edward Jacket

If you don't fancy dragging a tail coat around behind you, the Prince Edward jacket has a more modern feel, a three-quarter length jacket with a much less cluttered, single-breasted appearance at the front. The massive disadvantage is that it's woefully unsuited for shorter blokes, because it will just look like you're wearing a normal suit jacket but that it absolutely swamps you.

Frock Coat

Sometimes known as a Prince Albert, which of course is also slang for something else entirely, the frock coat is popular at weddings with a Victorian feel and typically drops to the wearer's knee-level.

According to weird etiquette rules they must not be worn past 7PM, but traditionally they were also worn by the Russian military, but that doesn't mean you're going to be dividing the church seating into 'blocs'.

One thing that people don't often realise is that depending on the cloth they're cut from some frock coats are really heavy and will leave you wanting to get rid of it as soon as possible. For this reason they make a spectacularly bad choice for a wedding at the peak of summer.

Turn to P72
to see Thomas Gunning rock the kilt

PHOTOGRAPH: FIONA KELLY WEDDING PHOTOGRAPHY

Tuxedo

These days, the dinner jacket/ tuxedo/tux/penguin suit is the key component of 'black tie' events. Such is the popularity of this look, we're entering a minefield here in terms of identifying what is, and isn't a dinner jacket. Typically, they're single-breasted, you'll almost always match it with a white shirt, and it will have minimal buttons which generally remain undone. Don't ask why they're there, the answer is too terrifying for you to comprehend. The tuxedo is an American wedding tradition for men, but that doesn't mean you can't opt for it at your wedding, especially if you fancy a themed black-tie bash, plus you can make loads of Bond gags. The other advantage is that lots of blokes already own a tux so you can co-ordinate.

Prince Charlie Jacket

Usually accompanied with a kilt and sporran (which is more of a wearable pocket, than a butch handbag), to the degree that we reckon it would look daft without them, this jacket of Scottish heritage is low and short cut for grooms who a) love to tease or b) have Celtic heritage. It's a specific little number that's also accompanied by brogues and a dash of heather in the pocket to complete the full Highlander look.

What to wear:
Essential Accessories

Once you've decided on your suit, you've got to run the gauntlet of choosing your accessories (BTW gauntlets are soooo last year). We're here to help you choose between your cravats and cufflinks, and maybe even smell better.

Top Hat

Perfect for hiding bald spots, but remember to remove when sitting or indoors, and definitely take your topper off during the service. Don't wear at a jaunty angle – it should be flat and sit about ¾ of an inch above the ear.

+ Lengthens the body and makes you look a bit taller, plus they're good fun if you've opted for the more traditional dress.

! Will make you feel like an Eton toff. Not necessarily a bad thing but it usually brings out a reaction in one or two. Quite easy to damage and lose, especially if used as a makeshift ice-bucket.

After Shave

Use the wedding as an excuse to experiment with a new fragrance (**http://bit.ly/AiU0hj**) and let's all agree that by the time you're married you should probably have moved on from Lynx...

+ Smell can be a fantastic aide-memoire and selecting a new fragrance you really love in time for your wedding can be a neat way of branding and capturing that time. Plus, you smell better, win-win.

! Test it out on the Mrs-To-Be first – you don't want her saying her I Dos while screwing her nose up.

Buttonhole

Buttonholes are a great opportunity to reflect some of your own style. Check out some alternatives to the traditional, yawnsome buttonholes
http://bit.ly/c5dRFW

➕ We've recently seen lots of grooms' parties wearing different suits but tying the group together with matching buttonholes. It's a great way of giving a team feel without going to the extent of wearing the same thing.

❗ Expect protests from the traditionalists.

Pocket Square

Brought back into fashion by Mad Men, your choice of how to wear a pocket square can really personalise your wedding look
http://bit.ly/98M3vn

➕ Pocket squares give your suit that extra touch, and allow personalisation between groom and groomsmen.

❗ If you produce yours with a flourish to come to the assistance of a tearful guest, just don't put it back in your pocket afterwards.

Watch

If your bride is looking to buy you a gift, you could mention a new watch. Alternatively, the fob watch look (see above) is very cool.

➕ Allows for an engraved message, looks great and is useful – it's the perfect present.

❗ If you want a top quality watch you're talking hundreds, if not thousands of pounds.

PHOTOGRAPHY: TOP HAT - ROSIEPARSONS.COM, BUTTONHOLE - SARAH GAWLER, POCKET SQUARE - EMMA CASE PHOTOGRAPHY, WATCH - MARK COLUMBUS PHOTOGRAPHY

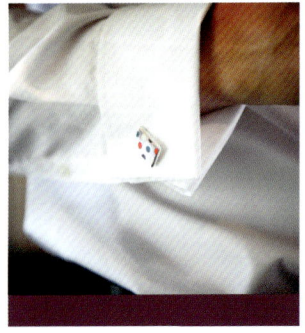

Cufflinks

There's a mind-blowing array of cufflinks. Check out Penrose London, Not On The High Street, Otis Batterbee, Stephen Webster, Tateossian. You should never consider buying ones with the word "Best Man" on them. Just. Don't.

➕ A perfect present, and a great opportunity to demonstrate your innate style.

❗ We're not kidding about the "Best Man" cufflinks. Seriously. Don't.

Socks

The wedding is the perfect time to set aside the Homer Simpson socks and investigate the classier end of Sock Shop.

➕ Another great present opportunity for the best man and ushers. With the advantage that a pair of designer socks will look great and not break the bank.

Shoes

You weren't thinking of writing "Help Me" on the soles of your shoes were you? The only personalisation you should consider is by having a look at **www.eshoemaker.co.uk**

➕ Find something comfortable. And ask a cobbler to set a strip of rubber in the sole if you find them too slippy.

❗ Don't forget to wear them in. Wincing down the aisle is not cool.

PHOTOGRAPHY: CUFFLINKS - BUTTERWORTH PHOTOGRAPHY, SOCKS - MARK COLUMBUS PHOTOGRAPHY, SHOES - SHELLY MANTOVANI OF TOAST OF LEEDS

Wedding Ties explained

If you're stuck on how to tie the various neckgear then take a look here **http://bit.ly/aQv11n.** First though, you should decide what sort of tie you want to sport on the day.

Tie – A simple tie, knotted in any of the 85 mathematically-possible ways to knot a tie.

Cravat – Much wider and fancier relative of the neck tie, which can also be tied in several ways, notably as a scrunchy tie or an Ascot (similar to cravat but simply worn under the collar).

Bow Tie – Once the geek's badge of dishonour, now sported by knowing hipsters and college professors alike. Essential with a tux.

PHOTOGRAPHY: TIE - THE BARBERS,
CRAVAT - WWW.HDMPHOTOGRAPHY.CO.UK,
BOW TIE - SARAH GAWLER

Real Groom

Dave Musson

Age: 25
Bride's name: Ellie
Best Men: Russell Fraser and Robin Mills

Where was your stag do – any scars?
I was never interested in having a stag do that involved me getting hideously wasted and ending up in all sorts of situations (and probably seeing me lose an eyebrow or similar), and my best men understood this, so much so that they actually asked me what I wanted to do! To kick things off, a group of us met at Halesowen train station before heading to the nearby Go Ape course on Cannock Chase. Being a primate for a few hours was fantastic, even if I did leave some skin behind on one of the Tarzan jumps.

What did the men wear on the day?
Suit shopping was the single most stressful experience of the whole wedding. For some reason, I decided it would be a great idea to take not only my wife, but also both my parents and her parents along to find the suit. We thought it might take half an hour or so... more than two hours spent traipsing round Solihull later and I'd had enough of suits! I also found out I'm quite an awkward size when it comes to suits that look right on me; I'm too skinny for my height and all the jackets looked odd. In the end, I found one that everyone agreed was right – a simple grey three-piece from M&S. The service was fine – almost as good as getting a pint as a reward afterwards!

What advice would you give to blokes going through the whole wedding thing now?
1. Decide beforehand what aspects of the day are really important to you and buy the best you can afford. For us, photography was high on the list – particularly given that I am a fledgling wedding photographer myself. Very quickly we settled on The Barbers, who did a superb job, as we knew they would.

2. When it comes to the speech – don't panic. While it may seem daunting, just try to write it without thinking too much and it should flow naturally. Also, if you want a good way of making it less intense, do what I did and propose lots of toasts. I toasted parents, best men, bridesmaids, absent friends and my new wife and it all seemed to go down well. It also means you can keep drinking mid-speech, which may help!

3. Don't be afraid to do something fun that doesn't involve the bride. Taking our inspiration from the wonderful world of 80s hair metal, me, my best men and a good friend from Uni donned big wigs, fake tattoos and spandex and formed our own covers band called Groomtallica. Everyone was told there were mystery guests on at 11pm and nothing else. It was, without doubt, the best gig I've ever played and was the perfect finale to the evening.

A word for the lady; come on, say something emotional about your bride...
I can't say enough about Ellie. We've been together since school, she is my best friend and she is beautiful, intelligent and amazing. I've never had any doubts about wanting her to be my wife and, now that she is, I can't wait to have the rest of my life with her.

How To Write Your Wedding Speech

Struggling to write your wedding speech? Can't think of the right words to say or how to get started? Don't worry, take a deep breath, get yourself a brew, a biscuit and some pens and paper because we promise* that by the time you've finished reading this article, you'll know how to write your wedding speech.

Calm? Composed? Then let's start at the beginning…

When it comes to writing wedding speeches (or indeed writing anything) these are the best words of advice you'll ever get:

Don't get it right, get it written

The first draft is just about finishing it. Don't worry if there are mistakes, there will be, but you'll correct them later. The key is to get a rough draft done before the panic sets in. So repeat with me: Don't get it right, get it written.

It's amazing but the age-old question of wedding speech nerves disappear when you're sitting on a great speech that you're happy with and all of that starts by simply writing it in rough. After that you practice it, run it past people and re-write it until it's perfect. Then you're confident and you can even enjoy delivering it.

Some basic information

- You should aim for your speech to be under ten minutes and ideally last between five and eight minutes. Even if you're a brilliant speaker 15 mins should be the absolute maximum.

- Before the big day have a meeting with all the speakers to discuss who's saying what and who is introducing you.

- If possible, practice with the mics you'll use or rehearse projecting your voice into the room you'll be speaking in – listen to others doing the same. It really helps to see the room you'll be speaking in, so you can imagine yourself there when you're practicing.

- See if the venue has someone who will act as Master of Ceremonies, or if there will be an MC. If not decide who will introduce the other speakers – it's often the task of the best man in the absence of a toastmaster.

*Like a friendly promise, not one of those legally-binding-i-can-now-sue-you sort of promises

Classic wedding speech formats

Let's look at the classic format for each of the speeches, in the order they occur in. Ultimately, you can just take these formats, flesh out the points and you'll have a perfectly decent speech.

Father of the bride

- Welcome guests and thank them for coming
- Welcome new son-in-law and his parents
- Talk about your daughter and say how you feel
- Toast bride and groom.

Groom

- Thank father of the bride for his speech
- Thank all relevant people (consult bride to avoid missing people). These are generally,
  - New inlaws (possibly for paying)
  - Your parents
  - Guests for attending and for presents
  - People who have helped with the wedding preparations (venue, florists, etc)
- The most essential thing is to talk honestly about how you feel about your wife, your relationship and your future.
- Toast bridesmaids
- (optional) Pre-empt best man speech

Best man

- Introduce yourself, thank previous speakers
- Talk about the groom (and the bride if you know her) – do this humorously but not destructively
- Give an outsider's perspective on the couple's relationship
- Toast the bride and groom
- Possibly read correspondence or hand back over to the MC

So what content do you put in your speech and where do you get it?

You might think that your mind is completely blank but once you've got to grips with the wedding speech etiquette, you'll at least have a rough idea of your content. Then it's a case of doing some research and starting to shape the material.

The more people you can get to help with your speech the better it will be.

- If you're a father of the bride, get your wife and other children involved. You could even ask the bride what she'd like you to say (you don't have to follow her advice obviously).
- If you're a groom speak to your fiancé about who needs to be thanked, ask her mates what sort of things they'd mention.
- As the best man you will probably have two or three good stories that demonstrate what sort of bloke the groom is. But once you speak to other people connected to him you could end up with 10 or 11 good stories to choose from, allowing you to pick the funniest material.

Especially for the best man's speech don't forget to include your fellow stags (pass a notebook round at the stag do, or use some post-stag emails), colleagues from his work, his parents and brothers and sisters, notable people from other places in his life such as people on the same sports teams or in the same societies. One person who best men often forget to talk to is the bride.

Good questions to ask these people are: what classic stories can you tell me about him? How would you sum up the groom? Has he ever said anything particularly funny? What is he well-known for? What makes him angry? Do they have any funny photos or material that they could send to you connected to the groom?

The other reason to speak to the bride is because not only will she have good material, she will also be able to fill you in on the important biographical information about their relationship that you might not know. You should find out where they met, how they became a couple, what sort of things they enjoy doing (without getting too graphic!) and how the groom proposed – whether he made a mess of it or if he was sweet about it.

An essential point on content

The most important thing for all of the speeches is that you should remember when it comes to gathering material is to ask yourself this very simple question: what do you want to say? This is the point in the day when you get to express your thoughts and feelings to everyone there. Ok, so maybe that's a bit nerve-wracking but it's also a tremendous privilege to be able to have that sort of opportunity, so use it – say something from the heart that people will remember.

It might sound obvious but we often get caught up in what we're supposed to say and forget that this is our chance to tell our best friend, wife, or daughter what we think of them. If the groom is a mate who has always been there for you - say so. If you couldn't be prouder of your daughter - declare it. If you're thrilled to be married to this beautiful woman - speak now! This honest statement of how you feel is the sort of thing that can make for the most effective toasts and it's what people will remember.

Once you've got your material

You should then consider the format of the speech. You might want to do something very traditional (introduction, few stories, toast) like the examples at the beginning, or you could want to do something more quirky and inventive. Either is fine but don't forget that the essence of a beginning, a middle and an end has worked as a structure for all of recorded history, and it will work for you too.

A word of warning. If you're going quirky – plan it properly and make sure that the format doesn't overwhelm the content, otherwise it's just showing off. If you have a lot of photos and videos that you want to use then you need to prepare well in advance. For instance you need to make sure that the venue you are going to has the correct audio-visual equipment for you to use.

Try and simplify things where possible – print out the photos onto a sheet of paper which you can distribute to the tables rather than projecting them. If you are using video then you need at least one rehearsal in the venue before the big day, to make sure you know how loud the video is, how to control the equipment and so on.

Once you have your material the next step is to sift through it and select the very best stories, the finest sentiments and put them in an order. For some inspiration take a look at the wedding speech library **www.iamstaggered.com/forum/wedding-speech-library** where previous grooms, best men and fathers of the bride have posted their speeches for you to read (and steal).

How to present your speech

- When printing your speech use a 12 point Arial font, which is formatted to have 1.5 line spacing as this is one of the easiest fonts to read when stood up.

- If you do this each page when read out should last approximately one and a half minutes.

- If you'd rather write your speech onto cue cards then that's fine but it's better to have a copy of the speech with you written in full on the day just in case your mind goes blank.

- Don't forget, your sweat-stained, note-covered speech makes a really nice keepsake/present. If you're the best man or father of the bride why not offer to frame all the speeches and, presto, you've got a simple, but incredibly thoughtful gift.

Don't forget

The classic mistake people make is to try and write the perfect speech at the beginning, don't. Just complete it and then refine it. It's so much easier to re-write something than it is to write it.

Ten Jokes We Are Officially Declaring Too Old To Use

1 Ladies and gentlemen, I am the best man, so in time-honoured tradition, I will do my best to give Dave the most uncomfortable five minutes of his life. For the record, the most uncomfortable five minutes of Sheila's life will be coming later on this evening, courtesy of Dave.

2 Public speaking isn't something that comes naturally to me. In fact, this is the fifth time today I've risen from a warm seat with a piece of paper full of crap in my hand.

3 Being asked to be a best man is like being asked to **** the Queen, it's a terrific honour but you don't really want to do it.

4 If I'm the best man then why is Sheila with Dave and not with me?

5 It's been an emotional day – even the cake is in tiers.

6 Sheila deserves a good husband. Luckily, you married her before she found one.

7 You've married Miss Right. First name, Always.

8 [Ask the bride to put her hand on the table, and then ask the groom to put his hand on hers]. Then say: "Savour this moment, because it's the last time the groom will have the upper hand."

9 To our wives and girlfriends, may they never meet.

10 Let us all be upstanding, and give the bride the clap she so richly deserves.

Still stuck?
Let us write your speech

It's all well and good knowing how to write your speech, but for some blokes it's a question of time. They simply don't have the days available to them in order to put together the perfect groom, best man or father of the bride speech. If you've found yourself in this situation, don't sit there panicking - let us write your speech for you.

Why choose us to write your speech?

The Staggered speech service is set up to give you access to the best speechwriters around. We've worked with all of these writers and know that they're brilliant, so from the beginning you're in very safe hands. We're so sure of this we're happy to provide you with a 100% guarantee. Staggered holds your money until you're completely happy with the speech. If you don't get a great speech you don't pay. Simple.

How does the process work?

You go to **www.iamstaggered.com/ wedding-speeches/speechwriters**, choose the speechwriter you want to work with and make sure they're available (do it quick because they get booked up!) The writer then does a consultation with you, over the phone and at a time that's convenient for you.

They then create a completely original draft and work with you to finesse it. Everyone who uses the service says that it's actually really good fun because you get all the quality with none of the work.

How long does it take?

Typically around a week from the consultation to the delivery of the final draft, but it can vary.

Isn't it cheating?

Googling for jokes and stories to pad out your speech is cheating. Working with a Staggered speechwriter gives you the speech that you would write if you had the time and were a professional speechwriter. You will get a speech that you will be proud to deliver, and there's absolutely no risk.

What now?

1 Visit **www.iamstaggered.com/ wedding-speeches/speechwriters**

2 Choose your ideal speechwriter and check their availability.

3 Book them and relax!

If you have questions email **speeches@iamstaggered.com** or call us on **0844 310 4050**.

The Team

The Staggered speechwriters are experts drawn from the world of stand-up comedy, screenwriting and, appropriately enough, speechwriting. Choose your favourite and put them to work.

Real Groom
Jon Solomon

Age: 37
Bride's name: Michelle
Best man: Hal Ewing

Where was your stag do – any scars?
I did the stag do in two parts. The first part I kept simple and cheap and just went for a night out in Nottingham. If you are not careful a stag do can become really expensive and I just wanted people to enjoy a night out with me – not worry about cost, using valuable holiday time or being away from family. Of course they dressed me as a woman (a nasty cross between Rocky Horror and Vera Duckworth!)

The second part was after the wedding – a GATS do. I wanted to make it an event – more than just a drinking session – so I wanted to go to a festival. We considered (Hal and I) the Bull Run at Pamplona, and La Tomatina... but instead opted for the Edinburgh Festival.

What did the men wear on the day?
Hal and I got our suits from Hugo Boss. I didn't want to hire one (not very personal), and what better excuse to splash out on a great suit that you can use again and again? I had free reign to choose the style and colour of the suit but did want to tie in to the reception and flower colour scheme – hence the matching tie and socks. Mich and I bought similar suits and matching ties for Mich's Dad and our nephews so that there was a trend through the wedding party – but not exact mirror copies.

What advice have you got for other grooms?
Make it your wedding. Loads of people are going to have their views on what constitutes a great wedding – or how it should be done (tradition gets bandied around a lot!)

Everyone will want something different – it is your day (not your parents), so stick to your guns. We decided three things early on and stuck to them:

1. People are there all day – no evening guests (I personally hate the idea of splitting people into 'good enough for all day'/'only good enough for the evening do'. We wanted people to be there for the whole journey.

2. No children except close family. We wanted our friends to enjoy themselves and let their hair down... not be distracted by children.

3. No faff – no favours (who wants sugared almonds anyway) no book to sign (some poor soul has to spend their whole evening trying to get people to bother) etc...

Get involved – blokes are classically not involved and I think that is a shame. Mich and I are a great team and we enjoyed working together on all the details.

Use Anna and Simon Clarke to record the day – they are great fun, cool, and take beautiful photos and video... it's a once in a life time day so get it done properly.

A word for the lady; come on, say something emotional about your bride...
Mich and I were friends and colleagues for about eight years before we finally got together. I loved her from the start but the timing just wasn't right. She is my perfect counterbalance and keeps me laughing, happy and feeling very loved... what more can you ask for (oh yes – I wish she would do the ironing a bit more often and wash the pots properly... but hey, you can't have everything!)

Dave Spikey's
Wedding Speech Q&A

Staggered has been lucky enough to have the BAFTA-nominated stand-up and actor Dave Spikey sharing his thoughts on wedding speeches with us and our readers. Here we collect some of his best advice to our readers

Help Dave I'm a groom and I'm not funny – what can I do?

The good news is that as far as I recall the groom's speech doesn't have to be that funny. The responsibility for a light-hearted and funny speech lies with the nervous wreck that is the best man. The groom's speech should be more sincere and heartfelt and include a mention to how beautiful your bride looks, thanks to various people who played an important part in the wedding planning, as everyone likes to be acknowledged in this way. I'm sure you will have a list of who these people are. But if you think they may be up for it there's still ways to get a joke in.

Thank the bride's father for his speech and for his beautiful daughter, maybe say that although he may not look it, he likes a laugh. Recount how nervous you were the first time that you were invited round for tea and when you got to the house he'd put a big sign in the front garden saying "Last Girl Before Motorway".

Tell them how you first met your beautiful bride – if you've known each other since you were kids maybe say how and when you first noticed she was blossoming into a beautiful woman. Maybe you first felt the attraction at school sports day when she was your partner in the wheelbarrow race and you had hold of her legs. You get the picture...

If it was much later in life tell of your first meeting and dates, there is usually something there that you did or embarrassed yourself saying or doing. Tell them about your chat-up line(s). Run through those you thought of but rejected to raise a laugh or a cringe – here's an idea – ask your mates for some of their favourites and on the day in your speech credit them with their suggestions.

Hi Dave, I've heard that you've got 10 seconds to win over an audience, is that true and if so what can I do in 10 seconds to make them like me!

I suppose that broadly speaking ten

to fifteen seconds could be make or break time but the situation is always redeemable. I would say that unless you make a complete idiot of yourself in your opening remarks there is plenty of time to win the crowd over. It's important to remember that a best man's speech is what you might call a home game because (I'm assuming) that you will know quite a few people present and they'll be willing you to do well. It's not the same as trying to win a room full of drunken, noisy strangers over in a late night comedy club.

Woody Allen said that his golden rule of stand-up was to make the crowd like you and I am a great believer in this maxim. No matter how nervous you are on the inside , no matter that you suddenly can't feel your legs and suspect that you might collapse at any moment, don't rush headlong into your speech, don't be overly enthusiastic, don't shout your hellos and "how are yous?" Get up and say your hello in a relaxed and friendly

way; comment on how beautiful the bride and bridegroom look.

It's important to remember that public speaking is still the number one fear in most people and consequently they will be on your side and will totally admire your "performance" if you deliver it with confidence , charm and humour – it doesn't have to be hilarious.

Hi Dave, I'm a bride and I want to make a speech but I don't know when would be best for me to make my speech?
Unless you're going to change the order completely the real question is should you insist on speaking before or after the best man? In case his speech is so funny it threatens to eclipse yours and, in doing so, piles the pressure on you. Having said that, on balance I'd go on after him, because the stronger argument could be that he'd warm the crowd up for you. Another big plus for this approach is that you've got the element of surprise on your side. I definitely wouldn't tell many, if any people that you intend to speak – the surprise should generate laughs and a very warm reception before you even start to speak.

To read more of Dave's thoughts on wedding speeches have a look at www.iamstaggered.com/category/ blogs/davespikey

Real Groom
Thomas Gunning

Age: 27

Bride's name: Rumana

Best man: Matthew Gunning

Where did you get married?

The church was situated in Bayswater – the same church in which my wife was baptised and where her parents were married, and the reception was in the Thistle Hotel in Marble Arch. The staff were amazing here and fulfilled our every need, so highly recommended for anyone planning their big day in the centre of London.

Where was your stag do – any scars?

For my stag do we had a weekend in Bournemouth. We competed in 'It's A Knockout', coming sixth out of 26 teams. I was almost drowned and dressed up as a bee. We also hit the clubs the pubs where we lost half of our group almost every night.

What did the men wear on the day?

Spirit of Bannockburn kilts. Being half Scottish, I wanted to wear a kilt for my big day. We chose Spirit of Bannockburn, not because it is my family's tartan but because it went with the theme my wife had chosen for the wedding! My brothers-in-law were anxious about wearing the kilts, with being from an Asian background they thought they wouldn't look right, but once they put the whole suit on – with the daggers and everything – they were impressed with the final

look! My gifts to my best man and ushers were boxer shorts with my mug shot on one cheek and their mug shot on the other; these were also worn on the day.

What three pieces of advice would you give to other blokes going through the whole wedding thing now?

1. Find ways of including everything you want on your wedding day – don't cut things out just because of expenses! Get friends and family to pitch in to help you create yours and your bride's special day.

2. Spend the night before your wedding with your family (dad, brothers, future brothers-in-law etc.) and close friends, and go easy on the beers!

3. When your beautiful bride is walking down the aisle, take a glimpse at her and then look away – trust me, it stops you from crying!

A word for the lady, come on, say something emotional about your bride...

I have seen many beautiful things in my lifetime but the moment I saw my wife-to-be standing in the doorway her beauty took my breath away and nearly brought me to tears. The realisation that I am spending the rest of my life with her was a truly amazing moment; not only have I found my best friend but someone who makes me a better person.

Plan the ultimate honeymoon

The precise reason why some grooms are left to book the honeymoon on their own have been lost to the sands of time (i.e. can't find it on Wikipedia). However, one survey suggested that as many as 31% of grooms are left to sort the honeymoon, so we've pulled together tips from specialists like Black Tomato and Sandals to help you get it right.

Speak to the experts

The key to a successful honeymoon is to have several surprises and gifts lined up for your wife throughout the trip. For planning on that detail you'll need help so speak to a specialist travel agent.

DO start planning the honeymoon well in advance. We'd recommend six months prior to departure so that you have plenty of time to chat through your ideas together or with a travel expert, secure availability and play around with the itinerary until it is literally perfect.

You are honeymooners, not holidayers

When booking venues and catering for your wedding, you may have been advised to play things close to the chest, to avoid incurring those sneaky little extra charges. The opposite can be true of honeymoon packages, with most suppliers getting in the spirit and throwing in some nice little extras.

Ensure that you look around for the best honeymoon packages, which often include gifts or upgrades. Also, always make sure the hotel is aware that it is your honeymoon, so that they are sure to make the experience extra special for you.

Book early... or late...
Tricky one, this: try to book as early as possible in order to avoid availability issues, or paying over the odds for your preferred dates. On the other hand...we're living in the age of LateRooms.com and last minute deals on cancelled flight bookings, so you may be tempted into a 'wait and see' approach. Fine, if you don't care where you go or when...

DO surprise her with something special. Even if she knows where you're going, it's a nice touch to plan a little surprise such as a hike before sunrise or a hot air balloon ride? Whatever it is, make sure you hold a little something back to surprise her with.

DON'T assume you have to 'fly and flop' on honeymoon. Yes, it's all about the sumptuous Egyptian cotton sheets and miles of white sand but you can still hike a mountain, swim with whale sharks or spot giraffes if you've always wanted to.

DO stay in amazing hotels. This is the one time you need to find somewhere incredible to stay, especially for the debut night. There are so many beautiful boutique hotels with authentic interiors set amidst staggering scenery; you just need to know where to look. For this, try a tour operator that knows boutique hotels, inside out.

DON'T assume flight upgrades are complimentary as standard. Unfortunately, this is becoming an incredibly rare occurrence for honeymooners. If you want to fly in first for the special trip, you'll probably need to book it.

Budget

Your wedding will have been an expensive time for you, and so it is a good idea to choose a honeymoon option which allows you to budget easily. All-inclusive resorts are a great option as everything is paid for in advance. Many all-inclusive resorts will also offer airport transfers, use of water sports equipment and a variety of activities– fees that can add up at a regular hotel or resort.

DO take some advice if packing her suitcase for a surprise honeymoon. This could result in near disaster, don't forget her underwear, swimwear, and footwear... in fact, definitely consult a close female friend. Or better still; book your bride-to-be in for a stylist day to kit her out for her trip.

DO consider a mini-moon and a bigger trip later on. Obviously it's a daft name, but mini-moons are becoming increasingly popular with brides and grooms taking a few days after the big day followed by a bigger trip a little later in the year. Why do one, when you can do two?

DON'T just book the exact same honeymoon your best mate found his bride-to-be. Make her feel special by putting a little bit of time and thought into proceedings, personalising the trip.

DO: Suprise her. Give the staff several small gifts to place in the room throughout your honeymoon. They don't need to be extravagant to make an impact, nor should they be "daily". Think a box of chocolates, some clothes, or sensual oil to use for... whatever you two see fit.

Keep things in perspective

It's easy to forget that the honeymoon is still real life and that means that if you are there 10 days, you might have a small spat. Instead of letting it ruin your trip (or even your day) suck it up, say you're sorry and move on.

Honeymoon:
Five alternatives to honeymoons

1 Have a staycation

Yes, it's a horrible compound word, but the theory behind it is solid: if you can't afford to go away for a holiday, bring the holiday to you. Stay at home, disconnect the phone, ignore the bills, lie in late, build a sandpit in the garden and – as the kids say – chillax. The housekeeping might be a bit lax though.

2 Take a weekend away

Honeymoons don't have to be long and relaxing. Consider a weekend-long city break to Paris, Venice, Prague or any of Europe's romantic hotspots. You could potentially plan in a year's worth of weekend breaks for the same cost as a single honeymoon.

3 Have a bumper funday

If time's the problem, think about how you can cram as much fun into a day as possible. Make a list of everything you'd like to do, where you'd like to eat and where you'd like to stay, get everything booked in and splurge on one unforgettable 24-hour bender.

4 Go camping

So it isn't the honeymoon suite at The Ritz, but a holiday under canvas is a great way of getting maximum holiday for minimum spends. If you want to keep some semblance of luxury, head for proper campsites with showers and toilet facilities. Camping's never the easiest holiday around but, hey, it's good to put the marriage through an early stress test.

5 Go to a music festival

With festival season now lasting all year, a life-affirming weekend of musical fun in the sun/driving rain could make for an unforgettable honeymoon for a music-loving couple. If the Vietnam-style conditions at Glastonbury don't appeal, investigate Latitude (**www.latitudefestival.co.uk**), Green Man (**www.greenman.net**) or one of the many European festivals for more sedate alternatives.

Real Groom
Dale Jones

Age: ...um, I'm guessing old won't cut it! I'm 42 and proud of it.

Bride's name: Rachel

Best man: I didn't have a best man, I can tie my own shoe-laces now and had a pocket to keep the presents in. My daughter was best girl and did a fine job of standing at the front of the church looking very pretty.

Where did you get married?

The ceremony was held in Kirkstall Abbey in Leeds just as night fell, led by a lesbian folk singer, who is Rachel's close school friend, and not even a proper vicar, despite the very convincing costume! It was attended by a small gathering of close family and friends. We made the ceremony up ourselves as we didn't want anything clichéd or over-used.

We had already exchanged rings at our legal ceremony in Las Vegas (helped ably by Elvis, who shimmied and shook while we said "I do") so instead of rings, we gave each other presents. After we had some fantastic photos taken we bundled everyone onto a red double decker bus and off to the reception at a small venue in Leeds (The Loft) where we had a champagne reception and BBQ and a cheese-free non-wedding DJ playing good old fashioned rock and punk all night. Everyone got drunk (that's traditional) and my wife and I were the last to leave after drinking the dregs of any bottle of champagne we could lay our booze-hound paws on.

What did the man wear on the day?

Hat from Village Hats. Card in hat from the Picture Machine tattoo shop in San Francisco, where I got a tattoo after our real wedding. Belt from a beach stall ran by a deaf guy in SF. Jacket from Living Dead Souls off the internet. Skinny jeans from Burtons. Fabulous shoes from Next One in Leeds (free after Rachel bought a Matrix leather coat!) Elvis shades from Elvis, of course, in Las Vegas.

What advice would you give to any blokes going through the whole wedding thing now?

It seems as though most grooms think the wedding day is all about what the bride wants when it ought to be about both people having their perfect day. When we started planning our wedding, the one thing we wanted to avoid was having anything that looked like most of the normal, traditional weddings you see every day. We are not a traditional couple and we wanted our wedding to be a reflection of who we are, not what other people think constitutes a wedding.

It is traditional for the bride to have a big entrance; not so much for the groom to get his share of the limelight. However, we didn't like this idea. So, I walked down the aisle first to Metallica's Ecstasy of Gold pumping out of a kick-ass sound system through a haze of dry ice lit with red spotlights. I looked awesome! Rachel came down the aisle after me, Yellowcard's You and Me and One Spotlight was her entrance music, and we said our vows. We ended up with the rock star wedding (or unwedding as it got nicknamed) by simply adopting the mindset of "it's our day so we can do what the hell we like." So we did.

A word for the lady; come on, say something emotional about your bride...

Hmm a bit about Rachel. Well you know the old cliché "you just know"? Well it was simply that. Hated being apart from her when we first started seeing each other and years later I still do, she means everything to me. Looking forward to getting old(er) together.

Meet the Staggered-approved companies who can make your wedding perfect

You can find photos, videos, background information and even some exclusive discounts for The Staggered Groom Guide readers. Simply locate their ads on **www.iamstaggered.com/suppliers** - see how much you can save...

GIFTS

Aimee's Boutique
www.utterlypersonal.co.uk

Beady Eye Designs
www.beadyeyesdesigns.co.uk

Bridal Designs Wedding Jewellery
www.bridaldesignsweddingjewellery.co.uk

Buy Our Honeymoon
www.buy-our-honeymoon.com

DOUZO
www.douzo.co.uk

Do Yourself a Favour
www.doyourselfafavour.co.uk

Julieann Beads
www.julieannbeads.co.uk

Le Trousseau
www.letrousseau.co.uk

Mai Pearls
www.maipearls.co.uk

OneBigPresent.com
www.1bigpresent.co.uk

The Gift Box
www.thegiftbox.co.uk

notonthehighstreet.com
www.notonthehighstreet.com/weddings

Paper Gifts
www.papergifts.me.uk

Zankyou.com
www.zankyou.com/uk

JEWELLERY

Brilliance Loose Diamonds
www.brilliance.com

Clearwater Diamonds
www.clearwaterdiamonds.co.uk

Crystal Jewels
www.crystal-jewels.co.uk

Gemvara
www.gemvara.com

Harriet Kelsall Jewellery Design
www.hkjewellery.co.uk

Hatlover
www.hatlover.co.uk

Iain Henderson
www.iainhenderson.co.uk/promotions/ staggered

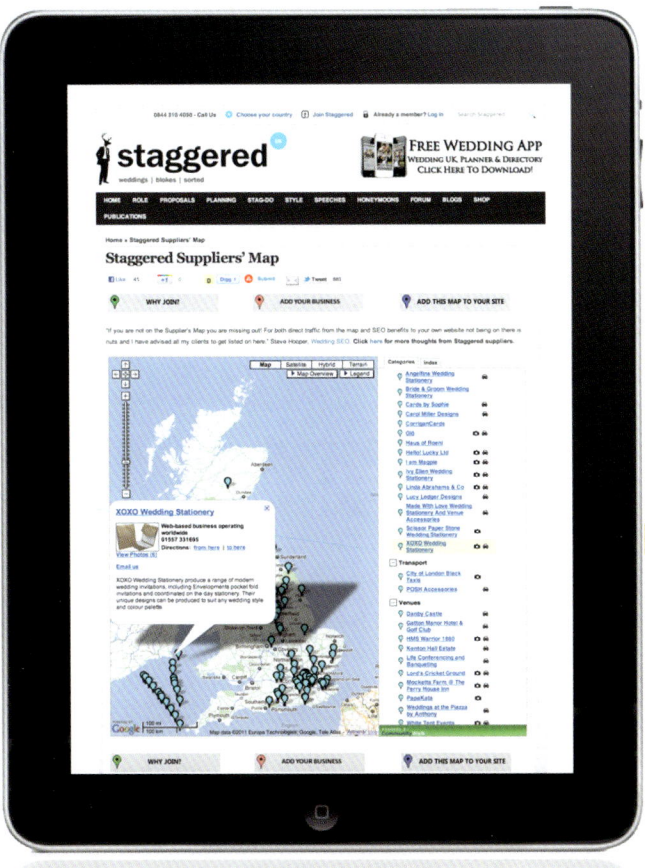

Visit www.iamstaggered.com/suppliers
to use our online suppliers' map

STEP 1

Click the legend button in the top right of the map

STEP 2

Tick categories you'd like to see suppliers for.

STEP 3

Click on the markers to see details, videos, photos & discounts

JEWELLERY

Ingle & Rhode
www.ingleandrhode.com

Jon Keith Diamonds
www.jonkeithdiamonds.blogspot.com

Jorgensen Studio
www.jorgensenstudio.com

Occasional Elegance
www.occasional-elegance.com

Rachel Helen Designs
www.rachelhelendesigns.com

ROCKED
www.rockedlondon.com

Rose Garden Accessories
www.rosegardenaccessories.co.uk

Seventy Seven Diamonds
www.77diamonds.com

Simply Jewellers Ltd
www.simplyjewellers.co.uk

Smooch Wedding Rings
www.smoochrings.co.uk

Stella & Dot Independent Stylist
www.stelladot.com/stem

PHOTOGRAPHY & VIDEOGRAPHY

20 20 Video
www.2020video.tv

Aardvark Wedding Films
www.aardvarkweddingfilms.co.uk

Adapting Light Photography
www.adaptinglightphotography.co.uk

Alan Abrams Photography
www.alanabramsphotography.com

AM Wedding Films
www.amweddingfilms.co.uk

Andy Garfitt
www.andygarfitt.com

Andy Wallis Photography
www.andywallisphotography.co.uk

Anneli Marinovich Photography
www.annelimarinovich.com

Anthony Williams Photography
anthonywilliams.co.uk

ARJ Photography
www.arj-photo.co.uk

Ashford Daly Photography
www.ashforddalyphotography.com

Babb Photo
www.babbphoto.photoshelter.com

Bad Little Bride
www.badlittlebride.com

Bartek Witek Photography
www.bwitekweddings.com

Beautiful Life
www.beautifullifeuk.com

Butterworth Photography
www.butterworthphotography.co.uk

Captivating Imagery
www.captivatingimagery.com

Chris Freer Photography
www.freerimages.co.uk

Chris Giles Photography
www.chrisgilesphotography.co.uk

Claire Evans Photography
www.claire-evans.com

Cocoon Photography
www.cocoonphotography.co.uk

Courtenay Photographic Ltd
www.courtenayphotographic.co.uk

Dave Musson Photography
davemussonphoto.com

Ask our suppliers if they do a discount for Staggered readers - most do!

David j Perkins wedding photojournalist
www.davidjperkins.com

Dean Hartwell Photography
www.deanhartwellphotography.com

Deneemotion Contemporary Wedding
HD Videography
www.deneemotion.com

Depict
www.depict-photography.com

Derek Anson Photography
www.derekanson.com

Dirk Van Der Werff Wedding
Photography
dirkvanderwerffphotography.blogspot.com

Envision Photography
www.envisionwedding.com

Exhibit Emotions Photography
www.exhibitemotions.com

Fiona Kelly Wedding Photography
www.fionasweddingphotography.co.uk

For Your Eyes Only Portraits
fyeoportraits.com

FourT4 Photography
www.FourT4.com

Gary Rowlands Wedding Photographer
www.garyrowlands.com

Get Knotted Photography
www.getknottedphotography.com

Gordon Tant Photography
www.gordontantphotography.com

Green Photographic
www.greenphotographic.com

Greyeye Photography
www.greyeyephoto.com

Hayley Ruth Photography
www.hayleyruthphotography.co.uk

hdmoments.com
www.hdmoments.com

Ian Bursill Photography
www.bursill.com

J.A. Photography and Video
www.janis-andrejevs.com/studio

James Davidson Photography
www.jamesdavidson.co.uk

Jean-Luc Benazet Photography
www.jeanlucbenazet.com

Julie Kim Photography
www.juliekimphotography.com

Jumping Spider Films
jumpingspiderfilms.com

Karen Flower Photography
www.karenflowerphotography.com

Kevin Mullins Photography
www.kevinmullinsphotography.co.uk

Lee Brown Photography
www.lsbp.co.uk

Lenzflair photography
www.lenzflair.co.uk

Marian McNeil Photography
www.marianmcneilphotograpy.co.uk

Mark Colombus Photography
www.markcolombus.com

Mark Osborne Photography
www.markosbornephotography.com

Mark Skeet Photography
www.markskeetphotography.co.uk

Marry Me Films
www.marrymefilms.co.uk

Martin Beddall Photography
www.mcbweddings.com

Matt Pereira Photography
www.mattpereira.co.uk

PHOTOGRAPHY & VIDEOGRAPHY

Matt Tordoff Photography
www.matttordoff.com

Mary Brown Photography
www.marybrownphotography.com

McAvoy Wedding Photography
www.mcavoyweddings.co.uk

my fabulous life
www.myfabulouslife.co.uk

PhotoGlow Photography
www.photoglow.co.uk

Pictures In Pixels
www.picturesinpixels.co.uk

Proof Photography
proofphotography.co.uk

Rachel Spivey Weddings
www.rachelspiveyweddings.co.uk

Randall Murrow Photography
www.randallmurrow.com

Raw Photography
www.raw-weddingphotography.co.uk

Richard Skins Photography
www.richardskinsphotography.co.uk

Sally Elvin Photography
www.sallyelvinphotography.co.uk

Sarah Vivienne Photography
www.sarahvivienne.co.uk

Simply Southern Photography
www.simplysouthernstudio.com

Struve Photography
www.struvephotography.co.uk

Suzanne Black Photography
www.suzanneblackphotography.co.uk

Tux & Tales Photography
www.tuxandtalesphoto.co.uk

Urban Bridesmaid Photography
www.urbanbridesmaid.com

Victoria Phipps Photography
www.victoriaphippsphotography.co.uk

Wedding Tales
weddingtales.co.uk

whitewithtwosugars
www.whitewithtwosugars.com

Wonderland Avenue
www.wonderlandaveune.co.uk

You Film Your Party
www.youfilmyourparty.co.uk

Your Perfect Day
www.yourperfectday.net

PLANNING

Aimee Dunne - Weddings and Events
www.aimeedunne.com

Always Andri Wedding Design
www.alwaysandri.co.uk

Barefoot Weddings
www.BarefootWeddings.com

Boutique Wedding
boutiquewedding.uk.com

Bristol Vintage
bristolvintageweddingfair.blogspot.com

Cerendipity Events
www.cerendipity-events.co.uk

Cherry Topped Bespoke Weddings
www.cherrytopped.co.uk

City of London Black Taxis
www.cityoflondonblacktaxis.co.uk

compare wedding insurance
www.compareweddinginsurance.org.uk

staggered APPROVED

Ask our suppliers if they do a discount for Staggered readers - most do!

Crystal Chair Covers
www.crystal-chair-covers.co.uk

Daisychain Events
www.daisychainevents.com

Dream Occasions
www.dream-occasions.co.uk

Element Event Design
www.elementeventdesign.com

EventAngel
www.event-angel.com

Glo
www.glosite.com

Heading Up The Aisle
www.headinguptheaisle.com

Helen Carter Weddings
www.helencarterweddings.co.uk

Hello!Lucky Ltd
www.hellolucky.co.uk

I am Magpie
www.iammagpie.co.uk

Isabel Smith Wedding Design
www.isabelsmithweddings.co.uk

Ivy Ellen Wedding Stationery
www.ivyellenweddinginvitations.co.uk

Just Bespoke
www.just-bespoke.com

Klass Act
www.klass-act.com

Knots & Kisses Wedding Stationery
www.knotsandkisses.co.uk

LilGuy Celebration Stationery
www.lilguy.co.uk

Linda Abrahams & Co.
www.lindaabrahams.co.uk

Love Scotland
www.lovescotland.com

Lucinda George Wedding & Event Design
www.lucindageorge.com

Made by Millie and Me
www.millieandme.net

Maple Leaf Weddings
www.mapleleafweddings.com

Mirage Weddings
www.mirageweddings.co.uk

NJ Vows Now
www.NJVowsNow.com

Pazazz Weddings
www.weddingplannerkentsussex.co.uk

Plans and Presents
www.plansandpresents.co.uk

PrivateFly.com
www.privatefly.com

Purple Grape Catering Ltd
www.purplegrapecatering.co.uk

Rattytatty Designs (Events)
www.rattytattydesigns.co.uk

Red Letter Event Planning
www.redlettereventplanning.com

Roseberry Weddings
www.roseberryweddings.com

Roeni
www.roeni.co.uk

Scissor Paper Stone Wedding Stationery
www.scissorpaperstone.com

Simply Elegant
www.simplyelegant.co.uk

Sticky Fingers Designs
www.stickyfingersdesigns.com

Ternevents
www.ternevents.com

The Glasgow Girls Wedding Guide
www.theglasgowgirlsweddingguide.com

Ask our suppliers if they do a discount for Staggered readers - most do!

PLANNING

The National Wedding Show
www.nationalweddingshow.co.uk

The Wedding Community
www.theweddingcommunity.com

Top Table Planner
www.toptableplanner.com

Weddings by Claire
www.weddingsbyclaire.co.uk

Weddings in Surrey
www.weddingsinsurrey.co.uk

Wedding Officiant
www.LeslieDavenport.com

White Grape Weddings
www.whitegrapeweddings.co.uk

XOXO Wedding Stationery
www.xoxo-wedding.co.uk

Your Day - Your Way
Weddings and Events
www.yourdayyourwayuk.co.uk

RECEPTION

Alex the Mind Reader
www.alexthemindreader.com

Bandwagon Productions
www.bandwagonproductions.biz

Booth Revolution
www.boothrevolution.co.uk

Cakes by Beth
www.cakesbybeth.co.uk

Cat's Whiskers Cake Design
www.catswhiskerscakedesign.co.uk

Crumbs! Couture Cupcakes
www.cupcakeslondon.com

Cupids Wish
www.cupidswish.co.uk

Delights by Cynthia
www.delightsbycynthia.com

Drawn Stories
drawnstories.org

Gorgeous Cakes
www.gorgeous-cakes.co.uk

Passionflower Design
www.passionflowerdesign.co.uk

PianoDJ.co.uk - Wedding Pianist
www.pianodj.co.uk

Pollen Nation
www.pollen-nation.co.uk

Prime Entertainment
www.prime-ents.co.uk

Rachel Jenkins
www.racheljenkins.com

Rainbow Delicious Bakery
www.rainbowdelicious.co.uk

Reaction Fireworks
reactionfireworks.co.uk

Redchurch Moments Ltd
redchurchmoments.com

Roses All Over
www.rosesallover.co.uk

Session One
www.session-one.co.uk

Snaparazzi Photobooths
www.snaparazziphotobooths.co.uk

The Wedding Calligrapher
www.wedding-calligrapher.com

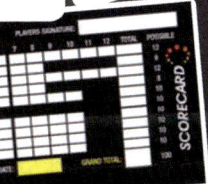

RECEPTION

Vayle Spring Flowers
www.vaylespringflowers.com

Why Are We Waiting
www.whyarewewaiting.co.uk

Yestercake
www.yestercake.co.uk

STAG AND HEN DOS

Action Boat
www.actionboat.co.uk

Airsoft Edinburgh
www.airsoftedinburgh.com

Apollo Spit Roasters
www.apollospitroasters.co.uk

Bantham Surfing Academy
www.banthamsurfingacademy.co.uk

Belle Vue Greyhound Stadium
www.lovethedogs.co.uk

Blue Friesian Ltd
www.bluefriesian.com

Campaign Paintball
www.campaign-paintball.com

Darkstar Ultimate Laser Arena
www.darkstarlaser.com

GO Ape
www.goape.co.uk

Glenkinchie Distillery
www.discovering-distilleries/glenkinchie

LetsGoActive
www.letsgoactive.co.uk

Lost Vegas
www.lostvegascasinohire.co.uk

Maskarade
www.mask-arade.com

National White Water Centre
www.ukrafting.co.uk

Perry Barr Greyhound Stadium
www.lovethedogs.co.uk/perry-barr

Pure Skill
www.pureskill.ie

Revolution Karting
www.revolutionkarting.com

Safe and Sound Outdoors
www.sasoutdoors.co.uk

Shaggy Sheep Wales
www.shaggysheepwales.co.uk

Slider Music Merchandise
www.slidermusicmerchandise.co.uk

Splash White Water Rafting
www.rafting.co.uk

The Comedy Cafe
www.comedycafe.co.uk

The Jungle NI
www.thejungleni.com

The Knights of Middle England
www.knightsofmiddleengland.com

The Makery
www.themakeryonline.co.uk

The Quadfather
www.thequadfather.com

Viking Line Cinderella
www.viking-line.co.uk

www.girlynightout.co.uk
www.girlynightout.co.uk

www.ladsnightout.co.uk
www.ladsnightout.co.uk

Ask our suppliers if they do a discount for Staggered readers - most do!

STYLE

Anthony Formal Wear
www.anthonyformalwear.co.uk

A Bespoke Design Ltd
www.abespokedesign.co.uk

A Suit That Fits
www.asuitthatfits.co.uk

bloom boxx
www.bloomboxx.com

Clements & Church
www.clementsandchurch.co.uk

eSHOEMAKER
www.eshoemaker.co.uk

Fabulous Tiaras
www.fabuloustiaras.co.uk

Goodrich Bespoke
www.goodrichbespoke.co.uk

Hugh Harris
www.hughharris.co.uk

IJORERE The Invitation, Inc.
www.ijorere.com

King & Allen
www.kingandallen.co.uk

Mia Sposa Bridal and Menswear
www.miasposa.co.uk

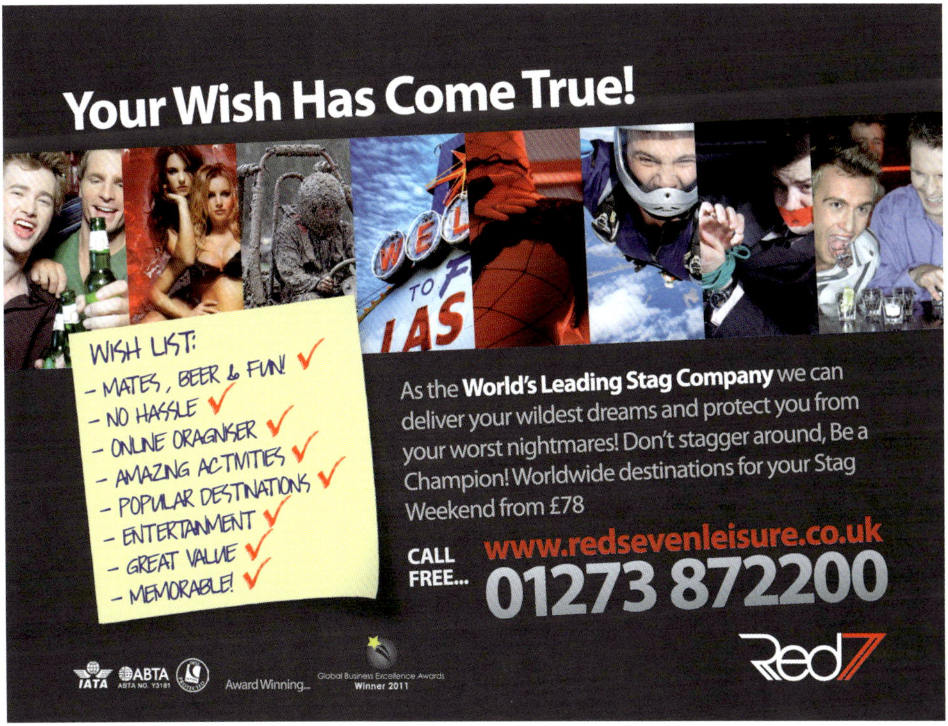

WE CAN DO YOUR STAG DO RESEARCH FOR **FREE**

Turn your vague plans into fully costed-out and booked stag do ideas with our help.

1 Fill out the form at
www.iamstaggered.com/book-your-stag-do

2 We do the research and get in touch with ideas and plans based on your notes

3 Book the perfect stag do and take all the credit!

Best of all, this service is completely free of charge for Staggered readers.

Ask our suppliers if they do a discount for Staggered readers - most do!

STYLE

My Tuxedo
www.mytuxedo.co.uk

PeakXVfitness
www.peakxvfitness.com

Skilt - Contemporary Kilts
www.skilt.co.uk

Suit the City
www.suitthecity.com

Swagger and Swoon
www.swaggerandswoon.com

Roses All Over
www.rosesallover.co.uk

VENUES

Danby Castle Events
www.danbycastle.com

HMS Warrior 1860
www.hmswarrior.org

Holiday Inn
www.hiwoking.co.uk

The Luxury Wedding Show
www.luxuryweddingshow.co.uk

PapaKåta
www.papakata.co.uk

Patrick Properties Hospitality Group
www.pphgcharleston.com

Lord's Cricket Ground
www.lords.org/weddings

Mocketts Farm @ The Ferry House Inn
www.theferryhouseinn.co.uk

White Media
www.whitemedialtd.co.uk

White Tent Events Ltd
www.whitetentevents.com

Want to get your wedding company on the Staggered suppliers' map?

Visit **www.iamstaggered.com/add-your-business**
and follow the instructions online

Real Groom

Kevin Donnelly

Age: 34
Bride's name: Jemma
Best man: Anthony Williams
Venue: Bisley Church

Where was your stag do – any scars?
My stag do was supposed to be a night of sensible, light drinking in Reading on 4th December. However, snow over the east of England put paid to it. So my stag do was me, a newspaper, several pints of Stella and a couple of bags of crisps – plain, I think.

What did the men wear on the day?
The dress code was black tie so it was black suits or dark grey suits with black neckties. In fact, because of the circumstances, it wasn't really a priority, so my best man's late arrival, in a blizzard, with his wife and children, was so wonderful and uplifting that his red bow tie seemed completely appropriate! My original idea had been for some kind of Jam circa 1980 look. However, although I did quite well on that front with a proper three-button mod type suit from Jeff Banks, I'm too old, too heavy and too bald to accurately represent Paul Weller in the Going Underground video. But it was the thought that counted.

What three pieces of advice would you give to other blokes going through the whole wedding thing now?
1. Be thankful for the wedding. I had no friends or family at my wedding, except for my parents, my sister and her fiancé and my best man, thanks to the oh so Christmassy wedding, and my parents only made it after a four hour journey from about 20 miles away. I, we, could have cancelled it or delayed it or just been really unhappy. But we made the best of it all and had a magnificent service and a fabulous day, made possible by the kindness of others and their determination to see our day. So, be thankful for what you have.

2. It is about the marriage, not the wedding. We had all sorts of things we wanted, but the key point was the moment of actual marriage. And when you think of it like that, everything else melts away and you realise what you are doing. Then you join yourself to this person and everything is different for ever.

3. Having said all that, the wedding is definitely the bride's occasion. You need to be prepared to give the bride most of what she wants because she will be doing a lot of the organising work – and let it flow over you. With a great suit you will look amazing, but it is different for girls (as Joe Jackson once sang).

A word for the lady, come on, say something emotional about your bride...
I decided, as the snow fell all around us, and the empty pews rang with the silence of missing friends and families, that what would make this most special was seeing her for the first time that day only when she walked up to join me by the altar. And the moment was incredible. She was, quite literally, the most beautiful woman I have ever seen, with an elegant dress, stunning headpiece, and a look of sheer love on her face.

THE GIFT LIST
SERVICE

A unique gift list service and the most
stylish ideas for your wedding day

NOT ON THE
HIGH STREET.
COM

weddings

www.notonthehighstreet.com/staggered

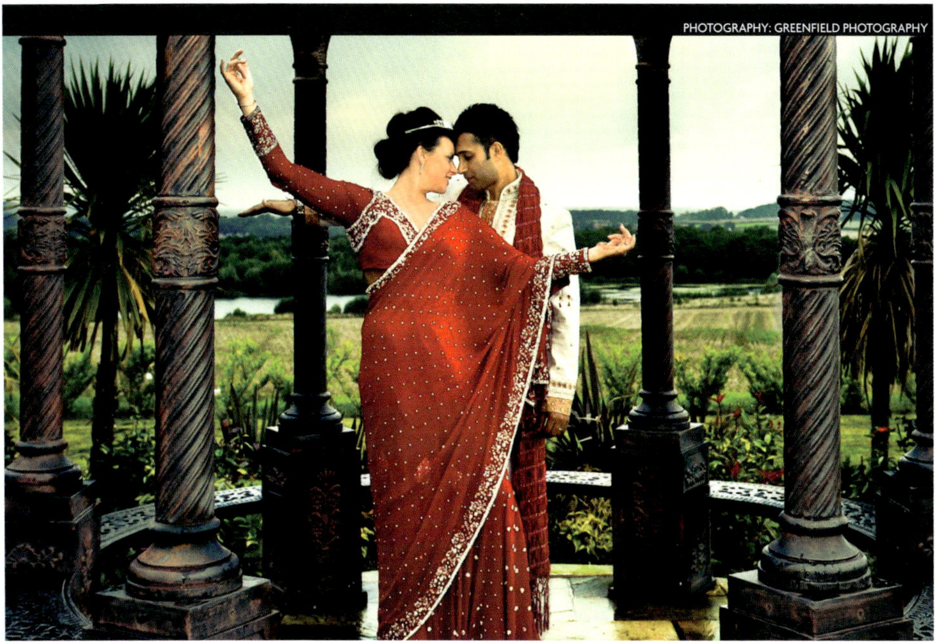

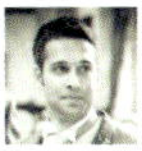

Real Groom
Vishu Passi

Age: 29
Bride's name: Nena
Best Men: Paul Day, Stuart Housley, Kushu Passi, Michael Staniland
Venue: Goosedale Hall, Nottingham.

What did the men wear on the day?
We got our suits from Pronuptia in Nottingham. My Sherwani was purchased from India, no less. My uncle has a shop in the Punjab called Billas Garments and he had them tailor made for us.

Where was your stag do – any scars?
The stag do was in Magaluf – 30 men strong descended upon the holiday resort. Let's just say, that there was a lot of drinking, a lot of fun, a lot of vomit, a lot of forced nakedness and, worst of all, a lot of sore heads.

What three pieces of advice would you give to blokes going through the whole wedding thing now?
1. For all the stresses and strains you're undoubtedly feeling now, it will all be worth it for the day itself and most importantly, your future together. Always remember that, especially when your wallet is empty.

2. Try and accommodate everything you can for your wife-to-be. It is a female's dream to get married from a young age. Therefore, as special as the day is to you, it is 100 times more so for her.

3. Take in as much as you can on the day as it will fly by.

A word for the lady...
I met my wife a few years ago in Birmingham. It was love at first sight! On top of being beautiful, she cooks brilliantly. Those qualities, on top of being selfless and passionate, are the perfect ingredients for the perfect wife. I am proud to call her mine.

WIN!
£2,000 of bespoke suits courtesy of Norton & Townsend

Norton & Townsend are one of the finest travelling tailors in the UK, bringing beautiful bespoke suits to the men of Britain. They've very generously agreed to offer one groom and his best man up to £2,000 to spend on their wedding day suits. With Norton & Townsend experts travelling across Britain (including Scotland) this competition is open to the whole of the UK. If you are lucky enough to win then you and your best man would have up to £1,000 each to create the most amazing suit you could wish for on your wedding day.

How to enter
All you have to do to enter is take a look at the Norton & Townsend website **www.nortonandtownsend.co.uk** and email the details of any Norton & Townsend offer to **norton@iamstaggered.com** including your name and contact telephone number.

Terms and Conditions: One winner will receive up to £1,000 worth of suit for him and £1,000 his best man. The competition will be drawn on 31/12/2012 - if your wedding falls before this date, you will still be eligible to claim the prize. Accessories are not included in the prize. Orders placed that total less than £1000.00 will not qualify for any other goods or cash. Any goods totalling over £1000.00 will require the relevant balance payment to be made. Only registered Staggered members will be eligible to win this prize. The judges decision is final. For a full list of terms and conditions please email info@iamstaggered.com Please add info@iamstaggered.com to your contacts to avoid our emails heading into spam – you might win and never find out!

PHOTOGRAPHY: BECKY AND NEIL BUTTERWORTH

Real Groom
Will Clark

Age: 27

Bride's name: Lauren

Best Man: Gary Clark

Where did you get married?

The ceremony was at Lauren's parents' village church in Lambley, Nottinghamshire and the reception was in Epperstone, Nottinghamshire.

Where was your stag do – any scars?

A weekend in York, with a group of my closest friends, hilarious from start to finish. We got to know each other very well over the weekend, especially when one of the stags walked into the communal room completely naked and started towelling down in the corner!

What did the men wear on the day?

I picked my own outfit which was all by Paul Smith, the three piece travel suit in blue, with a white shirt, silver tie and shoes. I even had matching socks! Lauren was pleased with my choice, she clearly knew that it would complement her dress perfectly. Lauren had left me a present on the morning of the wedding which was some heart cufflinks by Paul Smith. My best man and

ushers all wore the same slim fit navy suit by Next, with purple ties. Lauren's dad wore a navy Paul Smith suit. Everyone got brightly coloured and patterned cufflinks as gifts.

What three pieces of advice would you give to blokes going through the whole wedding thing now?

1. Remember to breathe when your doing your speech & your vows... It stops you from crying!

2. Keep something a surprise for your new wife; she will probably know all the details of the day and you'll be the one getting all the surprises.

3. I think etiquette probably says "get your bride a gift"... I didn't (but it's a good idea!).

A word for the lady, come on, say something emotional about your bride...

Lauren looked absolutely amazing in her wedding dress (not the dress I was expecting)! Her attention to detail showed through the whole wedding, and it was her little touches that made our day even more special for both of us.